18

FRAMES

OF

BEING

Published By
TALMID PRESS
New York City

ISBN # 978-0-9912108-0-0
Front cover photo & art by Bentzion Elisha
Back cover portrait by Steven B. Heiner

We are proud of this book.
Please send us your comments at:
TalmidPress@gmail.com

18

FRAMES

OF

BEING

RABBI
BENTZION ELISHA

TABLE OF CONTENTS

A Preface: The Writer's Introduction ix

1. Mental Museum. The Power of Perspective 19

2. Mountainside So(u)l 31

3. Jump into the Fire 57
Inspirations from a Farbrengen with Rabbi Yaakov Goldberg

4. A Child, On the Street, In the Night 79

5. Cleaning Lady Alert! 91

6. Gold and Silver 101

7. The Wealthy Family 107
A story from a Farbrengen with Rabbi Yosef Avraham Heller

8. Photosynthesis 113

9. The Answer for Everything 119
Inspirations from Farbrengens with Rabbi Chaim Shalom Deitch

10. Bloody Winter 135

11. The Human Camera 147

12. Seeing G-dliness 161
Inspirations from a Farbrengen with Rabbi Yaakov Goldberg

13. The King's Friend 185

14. The Art of Hugging a Tree 191

15. What Is A Farbrengen? 203
Inspirations from a Farbrengen with Rabbi Yaakov Goldberg

16. Our Purim Pogrom 215

17. Once upon a Customer 233

18. Making Enlightenment Last 239
Inspirations from a Farbrengen with Rabbi Yaakov Goldberg

Glossary 263

A Partial Publication History 269

Farbrengen Dates ... 273

Noteworthy Credits ... 275

About The Author ... 279

ଅଠଉର

BS"D

A PREFACE
THE WRITER'S INTRODUCTION

Dear reader,

This soul collage of experiences, stories and inspirations before you, is a compilation which comprises some four years of work on various short pieces of writings.

I've been privileged to have had many of these 'frames of being' publicized and published on popular websites and in print, made available to thousands of readers. (A partial publication history is included at the end of this book.) I am happy to unite these 18 cameos of life together in this humble effort, my first published book.

Unlike the previously published versions, I'm specifically choosing to include the complete and full versions of these stories and articles in my very own publishing enterprise, whereas certain parts and details were omitted in some of the printed renditions. I sincerely hope reading these 'organic' pieces with all their spice and flavor intact will enhance your overall experience of each and every article.

In case the meaning of the title of the book has eluded you, let me explain. 1) Every letter in Hebrew has a numerical value. The numerical equivalent of the word life is 18. 2) Just like a frame showcases a photograph or painting for display, literature can also showcase a picture or painting of life experiences and display them to others. 3) The word 'being' can be defined as a state of existence, a conscious existence or life. Another reason for the selection of this word is that it carries my initials, B.E.

This volume is made up of a grouping of 18, of life; frames, literary showcases for display; of being, particular points of and from my conscious existence. Hence the name '18 Frames of Being' for this anthology.

On this auspicious occasion, I'd like to share with you a Chasidic story which I was particularly enamored with, that I heard many years ago in Yeshivah by Rabbi Yaakov Goldberg…

ഇൽൽ

In the beginning of the formation of Chabad Chasidus by its founder, the Alter Rebbe, Rabbi Schneur Zalman of Liady, clusters of his Chasidim lived in various towns and villages in White Russia amidst tension and angst.

The new path of serving the Creator elevated the simplest to the most gifted Torah learner alike and threatened to revolutionize Jewish hierarchy as it was known. Now that the inner aspects of Torah were made accessible to all, each one according to their understanding via its thorough teachings, it jeopardized the authority of the non-Chasidic Torah scholars. Up until now they monopolized any esteem in the Jewish life landscape while looking down upon the common Jew.

Now secrets of Torah that were reserved for the elite few from an entire generation were made available and given to any Jew.

Chasidic teachings in general even turned the common Jew into a role model for purity of intent and honest egoless service of the Creator, also serving as examples to great Chasidic scholars. It redirected the emphasis of importance from a person's intellectual prowess to an individual's cleaving and devotion to G-d with all their being, mind, heart and soul.

The Chasidic way of Chabad in particular, utilized a person's mental understanding, wisdom & knowledge to grasp concepts of G-dliness, to cleave unto the Creator by way of cognitive familiarity, regardless of the individual's level.

In one such village where several devoted followers of the Rebbe Schneur Zalman lived, a scornful observer looked upon them with an unfriendly eye. As these simple people ascended in their goal of becoming Chasidim, he just grew in rage. He was certain he knew these people, personally, and surely they were no angels. He was convinced that they pretended to be more than what they really were. Who were these people fooling with their long 'heartfelt prayers'? Who did they think they were, learning Torah mysticism that even the great non Chasidic scholars of the region didn't know?

This man essentially had a good heart. He just kept to himself not bothering a soul; however his conviction finally drove him to action. One day he decided to put an end to these fakers' fantasy and finally wake them up from their misguided 'dream'. He was going to go to their Rebbe and reveal to him the true nature of his neighbors.

He traveled to the Rebbe and once there, he immediately made arrangements to reserve a private audience with him.

In their private meeting the man confronted the Rebbe. "Rebbe, with a sad heart I must inform you the truth about the situation in my town. Your Chasidim that live there are posers, they aren't real Chasidim, I know them. They fake davening for hours and pretend to learn your Chasidus, your mystical teachings, but these are just simple folk who are just making believe."

The Rebbe's face turned serious as he replied sternly, "Really? Is that really so?"

"Rebbe, it's horrible. They are pretending to be Chasidim but they aren't. They are just ordinary regular people" the man stated.

"Well then, let what it says in the Mishnah apply to them!" the Rebbe exclaimed.

The man was thrilled. Not only did he get the 'Chasidim' in his town in trouble, but actually he got their very own Rebbe to curse them! After the initial excitement, he searched his mind but he couldn't make sense of the Rebbe's curse.

"Rebbe, what do you mean? What Mishnah are you referring to?" asked the man.

The Alter Rebbe looked at the man with a piercing stare that seemed to go right through him as he answered. "The Mishnah I'm thinking of is the one at the end of Masechta Pe'ah, where it states that whoever is not lame or blind, G-d forbid, and pretends to be one in order to fool people into having pity and help him, will not die before he truly does become handicapped in the same condition that he pretended to suffer. So, you are saying that they are pretending; they are faking being Chasidim…Therefore let the curse in the Mishnah apply to them; they will not die before they truly do become real Chasidim!"

Instead of reprimanding these alleged 'posers' with a punishing curse, the Rebbe took the opportunity to transform the Mishnah's curse into a blessing to strengthen his students' efforts of becoming true Chasidim.

§0¢3

If we were to analyze this remarkable story, it is made up of Chasidim, a Misnaged and an encouraging masterful Rebbe. The Chasidim could represent a sincere endeavor or positive undertaking, the Misnaged could represent the negative nagging voice opposing a positive action, and the Rebbe could represent a strong encouraging supporter who enables the idea to come to fruition.

Embarking on anything worthwhile can arouse a discouraging voice at some point, whether from within or without (outside). However the negative voice, as convinced and convincing as it might appear, most of the time, isn't correct...

On a personal note, my writing and publishing journey, thus far, hasn't been without doubt and hesitation. However, thankfully with Hashem's help, the stories kept being published...

I must confess that I really had no intention of making this book. These stories just jumped into my life without invitation. In fact, some of these stories I sincerely wish I never experienced altogether. Although the subject matter of these writings are somewhat varied, they do share one thing in common. They all came about as a direct result of an urgent feeling of conviction that overtook me and literally drove me to write them down meticulously and share them publicly. Once I had a body of published work, it was through the strong suggestion and insistence of other people that I compile them in this stream of consciousness format which gave birth to this book and welcomed it.

Foremost, I'd like to express my whole hearted gratitude to the Almighty for enabling me to participate in the writing of these 18 literary works. It has been quite an adventure conveying real life stories onto paper and being the channel through which these writings came into being.

An extra special appreciation is extended to my father and my wife for their insights, comments, corrections and resounding confidence in me and my writings.

I'd like to thank the numerous friends and acquaintances who have proofread my works and helped polish these pages. I appreciate the time they have spent reading these works and their constructive feedback. I especially would like to acknowledge E. Fred Sher, Yossi Mandel, Chaim Baker and Shulamis Nadler.

I'd like to thank the Rabbis, whose Farbrengens I was fortunate enough to have attended and transcribe, for their inspiration and example. I'd like to take this opportunity to clarify that these Farbrengens were not edited by the Rabbis whose words I'm sharing. I tried to convey the information and inspirations they gave over to the best of my ability, however, I'd like to emphasize that if there is any mistake found therein, it is due to my own misunderstanding.

I'd like to thank the editors, websites and publications that have continuously published my articles.

Time after time, the publishing of a work strengthened my writing voice and encouraged further exploration of this expressive medium called writing.

If I were to personalize the story told above I would say that the Rabbis whose Farbrengens I've transcribed have definitely been the representatives of the sharp encouraging voice of the Alter Rebbe in my personal life. If I were to use the analogy a little bit more loosely and relate it to treading a new path in general, the role of the Alter Rebbe in the story could be the encouraging proofreading of friends, editors, websites and publications who published my works. They positively enabled me to overcome inner doubt regarding proceeding on this path of writing and publishing which pushed me to take step after step forward.

May Hashem bless all the people, and their families, who assisted in any way in the publication of my writings in general, and the production of this book in particular, with infinite blessings in all realms, both physically and spiritually.

Upon the publication of my father's first book he chose to dedicate it to his parents. A bewildered secretary of his asked him why he chose to dedicate it to his parents and not to his wife and children. My father's simple reply was that he met his parents many years before he met his wife and kids!

Beyond what words can express, I am and will always be indebted to my parents' constant nurturing and positive support. May Hashem bless them with a long, meaningful and healthy life, Nachas from all of their descendants and much success in all of their pursuits.

Alas, despite this family history, I am inspired to change course from my father's (first book) choice of dedication...

I am honored to dedicate this book to my personal Eishes Chayil, woman of valor, my esteemed wife!

Thank you for partnering with me on the voyage of life. May Hashem bless you in all ways possible with revealed goodness and kindness, catapulting you always from strength to strength. May you continue to be a luminous example for our children, and to all around you.

May Hashem bless us (and our children) with a Binyan Adei Ad, Shalom Bais, Dor Yesharim Yevurach, Nachas, Hatzlacha Rabba, perfect health and a long meaningful life, together, beyond one hundred and twenty years, with the holy Shechinah, the Divine Presence, always in our midst...

Working on these articles has been a labor of love, throughout which I strongly felt its importance. Although rewarding, it has been a long and tiring process to bring each work individually, and the entire collection collectively, to their completion. Nevertheless, I will not delude myself or you by presenting myself as 'a writer'. I do hope, though, that somehow, through the efforts exerted so far and through future ones, I will tap into the words of the Alter Rebbe (even if they aren't already there, they will become...) and, with Hashem's help, in addition to the merit of becoming a true Chasid, enhance people's lives by becoming a true writer, and publish more literary works.

My ambition for these pages is to elevate the content inherent in your (and my) 'frames of being' to greater heights of consciousness. I truly hope that your voyage through these stories will be most enjoyable. In addition, I would like to sincerely thank you, dear reader, for picking up this book and reading it with an open mind and heart.

I pray that this personal offering will be a contribution, if only a slight one, to the hastening of the imminent complete redemption.

Bentzion Elisha

The 5th of Menachem Av, 5774; August 1st, 2014.
The day of passing of the Ari HaKadosh.
Erev Shabbos Chazon; the day prior to the
'Shabbos of Vision.'
Brooklyn, New York

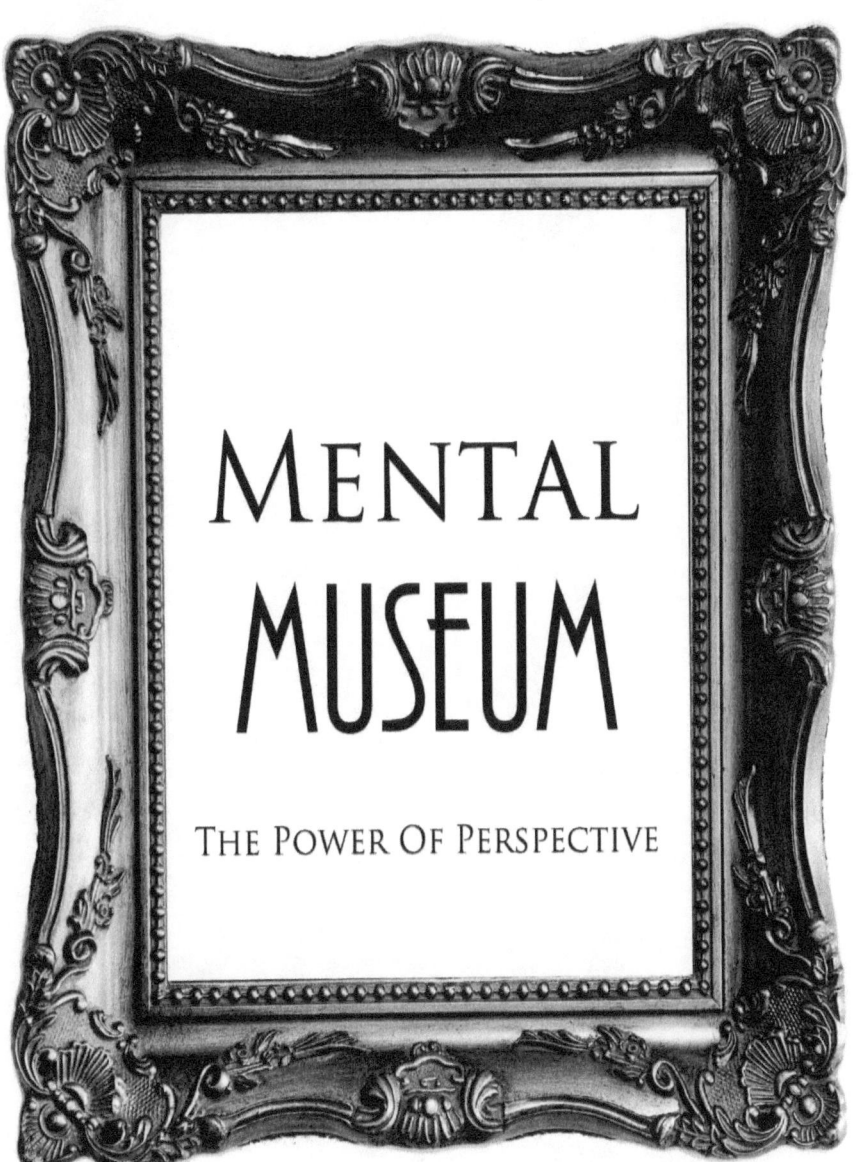

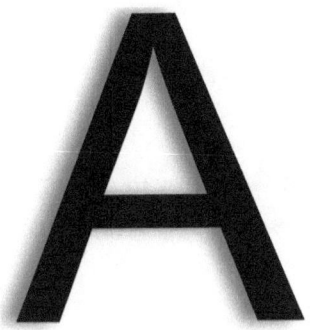young medical student was visiting a mental asylum as part of his training. One of the patients that he met there was a passionate twenty-something man with whom he struck up a long conversation. The long dialogue helped convince the young doctor in training of the young man's mental health.

He was so impressed with the patient's etiquette and seemingly high level of education that the doctor decided to help free the young man from this dismal place. Surely placing this fine young man in the institution was a grave mistake... The doctor vowed to the patient right there and then to help get him out.

As the young student was exiting the area, he fell to the ground from a strong sudden impact to his head.

Bleeding on the floor from a stone hurled at his head, he picked himself up and looked back. To his utter amazement the stone thrower was none other than the man he promised minutes before to help free!

As their eyes met, the man innocently asked the young medical student "You won't forget to help me get out of here, will you?"   *(As heard from Meir Rhodes)*

Sometimes we can be hit with the realization that our perspective was completely off...

ೞಸಿಲ

A peculiar childhood story that was repeated to me several times by my father, illustrates the importance of perspective...

A ruthless emperor desired to have a portrait of himself painted by a famed artist. The artist was handpicked by the court for his exquisite renderings and once hired, he embarked on the task at hand, which was to make a true masterpiece featuring the glorified emperor.

When he finished his fine portrait, the artist took great pride in presenting the work to the ruling emperor.

Contrary to the expectations of the artist, the painting was greeted with anger, annoyance and disappointment by the fuming emperor.

The verdict was simple, "Kill him!"
"Why kill the artist?" The court advisers asked the ruler.

"With his painting he is making a fool of me! " The emperor explained that the vantage point the artist decided to depict highlighted his handicap, his amputated leg, of which he was embarrassed.

"People will see this picture and laugh at me!" The emperor concluded.

When the court found another worthy artist he was already warned of the previous artist's fate.

Fearing for his life, the artist portrayed the emperor standing tall and strong on two healthy legs.

Confident of the painting's approval, the artist was taken aback when the emperor was angered by his stunning portrait.

Under his heated breath the words that were heard were, "Kill him! "

"Why kill *this* artist?" The court advisers asked the ruler.

"With his painting he is mocking me! This idealized picture isn't really me. This artist's perspective is making a joke of who I really am! "

After a long search the court found a third artist of outstanding talent. Despite being seriously warned of certain death if his portrait will not be accepted by the emperor, the artist took on the job.

After several months of hard work the painting was complete. The court was sure this artist will be killed just like the other two artists.

When the artist presented his masterpiece to the powerful ruler, everyone was shocked. This time, the emperor smiled and declared the painting a great success!

How was this work different than the other two?

The third artist, forewarned of the previous attempts, knew not to make a painting that revealed the emperors handicap and he also knew not to idealize him.

He ingeniously painted the emperor on top of a horse with his healthy leg showing while the amputated leg was on the other side of the horse, hidden from view.

The artist's chosen angle of view simply emphasized the positive by painting the good side while the negative was left out.

ಬಿ೦ಆ

As the famous saying goes, 'perspective is everything', but what is it exactly? While looking for a definition for the word perspective, three stood out:

1) All that can be seen from a certain point. (Merriam-Webster.Com)

2) A way of looking at or thinking about something. (Merriam-Webster.Com)

3) A particular evaluation of a situation or facts, especially from one person's point of view. (Bing.Com)

There are other definitions of perspective that relate specifically to art and the appearance of depth and distance of the portrayed objects, nevertheless, all these above mentioned definitions could also apply to the visual arts.

In painting, photography, and cinematography, the angle of view will affect the mood, feel, and content of the image or story portrayed. Changing the vantage point will alter the entire outcome.

Everyone is welcome to participate in the vast enjoyable world of art and the creative process. However, a piece of art could be made in a way that doesn't satisfy, not the artist (or wannabe artist) or, needless to say, the viewer.

Nevertheless, some are celebrated for their unique perspectives that are fresh, original and/ or beautiful.

ಬಿ೦ಆ

Perspective personally relates to us since everyone is an artist. We are actively creating art of our everyday life experiences whether we know it or not.

In addition we are curators of our own museum, our renderings are kept in one's mind, 'the mental museum.'

Sometimes we produce 'paintings' that we painted depicting the people and world around us slowly developing over an extended period of time.

Sometimes we take 'photographs' that we snapped in a split second, a quick impression.

Both are constantly shared with those who we invite into our personal museum, our sphere of being, by speaking with them and sharing a piece of our mind.

Taking bad photographs or painting awful paintings and exhibiting them is easy and requires absolutely no thought or effort. However, once they have taken unflattering snaps of their world and its peoples, the artists are left with toxic negativity towards their subjects because of the images they themselves have taken, which polluted their view.

The challenge and responsibility both in art and the art of life is to produce the best imagery possible. For that, deliberate effort has to be given and energy has to be spent. The rewards though are infinitely positive even in the most mundane of experiences.

(What makes for a good image is a subject for debate, however even the most 'realistic' depictions that don't attempt to make a flattering image must have a visually stimulating aesthetic on some level, whatever the subject matter. Exaggerations, whether positive or negative are just that, exaggerations, however accentuating positive points seems more desirable than accentuating the negatives in most art forms.)

ഇൻൽ

To illustrate the power of perspective, let me share with you a couple of personal stories:

Just several weeks before she died, my wife's grandmother called us, my wife and I, before Rosh Hashanah to wish us good tidings for a good and sweet new year. At the time she had suffered from a serious illness for a few months.

I took the opportunity to ask this dynamic lady, who had lead a very full life and exuded charm, wit and life experience, what would she say was her key to life.

What was her 'secret' for smart good living?

She replied immediately without any hesitation, "The key to life is encapsulated with three words. Two of them are 'think positive' and the third is 'prioritize'."

Thinking positive made sense to me, but 'prioritize'?

"What do you mean by prioritize?" I asked her.

Explaining herself she said, "Look at me, here I am suffering from a life threatening disease. I know the situation I'm in, I'm not delirious, however, if I wasn't positive I'd be depressed bringing myself and all those around me down. I don't want that for myself. That isn't my priority. My priority is to relish every moment I have, and enjoy my living. I am very thankful for every day, every moment. This appreciation is my priority!"

For me, 'the key to a good life' learned from my wife's grandmother is all about cultivating a positive perspective.

In her opinion, for a good life, it's vital for a person to think positively, meaning to say that generally a person must seek a pleasant outlook on life. In addition, it's crucial to prioritize, which means to consciously choose to concentrate on the best viewpoint of any situation. Alternatively these two things, prioritizing and thinking positive, could be a formula, first decide to look at the good of a situation in general and then find the best vantage point or points to experience it through.

A second story gives us a glance at the power of perspective from yet another angle...

Recently I witnessed an interaction between two individuals who regularly argued and contradicted each other freely in their conversations, about almost everything.

This time one's comments revealed the image they had of the other which was less than flattering. Somehow this time it was more apparent than other times because of how it manifested, however this hidden image could always be detected under the surface in many of their dialogues.

Knowing both, I knew that this character assessment was off, not just now, but in general.

He was being stereotyped by the other's negative ultra-pessimistic world view that always found fault with anything and everyone.

An interesting metaphor jumped to the forefront of my consciousness soon thereafter. This misperception resembled someone who was taking pictures of someone and got a rare photograph of them falling.

Not only did he choose to keep that one unflattering portrait depicting them in a fallen state, but he prominently displayed it in his 'mental museum' for all to see. Mind you, this individual falls very seldom, however the only image his friend carried of him was this one.

The person was always being depicted as failing in the other person's mind unfairly. The only perspective that was preserved and displayed was a negative one.

Needless to say, holding on to this view of the person, did not increase the peace between the two...

This happens every day to almost everyone in varying degrees, by us and to us. We should be aware of this phenomenon, and be aware of any unjust outlooks and renderings of others by us, consciously or unconsciously. Before we can produce a truly beautiful picture, we must first reject the option of using a bad or negative perspective.

ଽଠଔ

Harnessing and utilizing the power of perspective is of the utmost importance. Hunting for pleasant perspectives and finding the most positive and aesthetic angle of view surely will catapult the status of our inner museums and introduce escalating well-being.

These above mentioned stories could be encapsulated into 'The Rules for Better Perspectives':

Reposition. The situations and people around you are more than they seem. Reposition yourself to get a different perspective than the limited one you've acquired previously. Experiment and discover the best angle.

Accentuate the positive and avoid the negative (it's toxic!). Highlight the best aspects of the scene before you. Leave out anything unflattering or demeaning. Everything has advantages and disadvantages, as an artist in life; your goal is to reveal the good.

Think positive and prioritize positively. Results are outcomes of a person's outlook. Take charge of your perspective and keep them up and positive. What you choose to invest your energy in, this attitude or that, affects your entire being. Prioritize to appreciate the uniqueness of the moment and celebrate the specialness of the individuals you encounter. Make the most with what you have and with whom you spend time.

Contributing 'pictures' with better perspectives to our personal 'mental museums' will surely elevate the global gallery, ultimately improving 'the big picture' tapestry of the world.

We must push ourselves to be the best 'artists' we can possibly be. Our life depends on it...

೮つಀ

TWO RABBINIC STUDENTS ENCOUNTER THE WILD WEST...

S omewhere between heaven and earth, on the picturesque mountainous terrain of Aspen, Colorado, I'm in the car, waiting.

Dovi stepped into a store before we leave this plush resort town and he is taking his time, which is fine with me.

Staying by the Shliach over Shabbos really helped us. The lump sum of money we got for this summer 'soul searching trip' to Colorado from our Brooklyn home base was tight, to say the least. The money we saved will sure come in handy for the continuation of our expedition.

Having lost track of time on the downtown Denver streets Friday, finding Jews to inspire, we decided to take a risky shortcut to get to Aspen on time. We managed to 'get lost' and somehow passed through Leadville, the highest incorporated city in America, standing tall at 10,152 feet.

While asking for directions, we were warned that the passage to Aspen could be problematic since it might be snowing in that area and therefore the road could be blocked. We took our chances which meant we would be going through winding fenceless roads with scary cliffs by their side, steeply tapering several thousand feet straight down. We passed Mt. Elbert, the tallest peak of the Rocky Mountains which looked pretty snowed under from a distance.

The slow speed we had to drive down these snakelike paths heightened our anxiety since we had to get to our destination before sundown. The thought of not making it and being forced to make Kiddush on bottled water and feast on canned tuna inspired us to want to accelerate our speed, but the speed signs and deadly cliffs kept us crawling at fifteen miles per hour.

Dovi every once in a while would shriek since I was driving and taking pictures at the same time, our car was repeatedly just a few feet away from the edge...

The clouds underneath us and the frozen snow which created masses of ice by the roadside, even though it was summertime, reminded us how high we really were.

Other more painful reminders were the constant headaches and dizziness caused by 'high altitude sickness.'

We only arrived in Colorado on Wednesday and clearly we haven't acclimatized to the high grounds.

Since our arrival we felt terribly sick and our kind Denver hosts shared with us that no, it wasn't something we ate, but rather we aren't used to the high altitude which can give people the 'bends.' The only remedy was drinking a lot of water to ward off the symptoms.

This advice saved us, especially on this trip to Aspen, since our chosen shortcut went through such extreme heights which just intensified the sickness. We literally drank a bottle of water every five minutes otherwise we would feel the severe headaches coming on pretty quickly...

Ironically enough, when we finally did arrive at the rabbi's house, just before Shabbos came in, our welcome was a rather frantic one. The rabbi's baby was suffering from the same acute mountain sickness we were troubled with, since the baby had just travelled to New York with the mother and didn't reacclimatize yet since their return.

It was a very pleasant Shabbos but now it's Sunday, and the road is calling us.

Dovi and I, two rabbinic students from Tomchei Tmimim Yeshiva in Brooklyn, had Jewish souls to kindle on the mountains of Colorado and the open spaces of Wyoming. We were sent here on a holy mission to inspire.

I make use of the time waiting for my colleague to fill out the log book we are supposed to keep, documenting our spiritual work. I open a bottle of water to keep the headaches at bay and sip as I prepare to write. The image of the young man we met in downtown Denver on Friday comes to me.

His kind demeanor and politeness was eerily accompanied with his unusual habit of dozing off in the middle of our conversation. He was hanging out with an older looking friend who was shamelessly lying down by the sidewalk on the big shopping strip resting his head on a knapsack.

They both gave off derelict energy. I also suspected that they might be homeless.

When we walked past them, his friend's loud call to us initially was a little alarming; however, his mellow friendliness assuaged any concern we might've had.

Apparently a Jewish family helped him in his youth when he was down and out and nobody else did. He remembered their kindness to this day.

Unfortunately, he still was downtrodden.

We asked him if he was Jewish and he said he wasn't, however, the younger man with him was, he mentioned.

Our interaction with the Jew was aided by the non-Jewish friend. When we offered the Jew to put on the Tefillin, his friend urged him to do it.

Once he agreed, I must confess that I felt more than a little uneasy about it, because he appeared to be high on drugs. Nevertheless, the whole purpose of our being there was to bring merit to Jews by performing a Mitzvah.

He seemed harmless enough though as he pitifully nodded off again and again. As he rolled up his sleeves I was queasy and afraid to look at his arms. I really didn't want to encounter any needle marks…

I sighed of relief when I discovered he was 'clean' of any markings. I placed the Tefillin on his arm and he repeated the blessing after me, after which I proceeded to wrap his arm with the strap. I put the head Tefillin on him and he said the 'Shema'. He nodded off a few times during this Tefillin wrap; however, he was visibly touched when conscious.

When we finally finished, he sat down on the curb and his nodding off gave way to deep sleep. The whole while, Dovi tactfully navigated the conversation with his usual sleek charm and humor, even though the whole interaction was a rather sad one.

How tragic I think to myself. It isn't easy to see someone down and out on the street, both spiritually and physically...

The gentle gentile thanked us for caring for his Jewish friend and enabling him to do something Jewish. We bid him farewell, however we didn't get a chance to say goodbye to the Jewish man, since he was fast asleep on the curb clearly under the influence.

Before we continued on our way looking for more Jews, I left some Jewish literature in the young Jewish man's backpack about the upcoming Jewish holidays. I was hoping that maybe when he wakes up he'll read them, with G-d's help. Praying that he will be inspired to really 'wake up' from his sedated state of being.

I enter this meeting in our log book. I sit back in my car seat and gaze out of the windshield into space, thinking. Then, waking me out of playback mode, Dovi reappears with a friend...

"Bentzion let me introduce you to Sol." Dovi says.

I exit the vehicle after placing my log book down and smile as I greet him.

I quickly size up this youthful twenty something. Sol is dressed in baggy, dirty, hippy clothes and is wearing a backpack. An unpleasant odor surrounds him, revealing that he hasn't taken a shower for some time. His long reddish dreadlocked hair is semi covered with a knit cap. His speech is easy going and on the mellow side.

"How did you meet each other?" I inquire.

"I was in the restroom and I was surprised to see someone wearing a skullcap, a Kippah" Sol started explaining as Dovi finished off the thought..."Then he pointed at me and said 'you're Jewish! I'm also Jewish'."

"That's so unusual. I thought you were going to take a personal break, meanwhile I see your Kippah never rests, and works harder than you..." They both smile at my attempted humor.

"So what are rabbis like you doing in a place like this?" Sol asked.

"Well we actually came thousands of miles especially to meet with you." Dovi quickly quips as Sol makes a disbelieving face.

"He isn't kidding," I explain further. "We are students from the Lubavitcher yeshiva, Tomchei Tmimim, in Brooklyn. In the summertime there is an interesting training program called 'Merkos Shlichus' which sends rabbis in training to areas all around the world in pairs to meet Jewish people and hopefully make a soul connection. Help perform a Mitzvah, schmooze together, to bond with Jews in the world wherever there isn't an official Shliach. This summer we are part of this program which sent us here."

"Hmm, interesting but what's a Shliach?" Sol asks.

"A Shliach is an emissary of the Lubavitcher Rebbe. A Shliach is a Chabad rabbi and his wife who are sent to a certain place to motivate Jews to elevate their experience of Judaism, just like us, only permanently."

"Oh yeah, we had my Bar Mitzvah with a Chabad rabbi back in L.A where I'm from." He reflects thoughtfully.

His eyes narrow a bit and refocus on our car behind me.

"Looking at your car you must be sent with buckets of money" Sol sharply remarks.

"I wish. We're actually on a very tight budget. There's a little story behind how we got this car." I look at Dovi knowingly before I proceed.

"We are going to be on this road trip for 18 days and I had to make sure not to overspend on a rental car being that I'm in charge of managing the money for this endeavor. The money should cover airfare, lodging, food and of course the car rental. The car I thought most appropriate for the amount we could spend was the smallest and cheapest vehicle. As we arrived at the Denver airport car rental station, Dovi discovered the car I had reserved and he absolutely refused to accept the situation.

There was friendly lady by the desk and Dovi explained to her that we had arrived for a very important spiritual mission. He then completely shocked me when he promised her that we would pray for her children if she could look into her computer and try to help us out... I was even more shocked when she looked him in the eyes and seriously said that she would see what she could do, propelled by his words. She immediately started typing up a storm and came up with something. When the airport bus stopped by our vehicle we couldn't believe our eyes! The lady hooked us up with a brand new spacious Subaru Outback station wagon. It must've cost at least double what I reserved. We've been praying for the lady's children ever since!" `

"That's just unbelievable!" Sol declares bewildered.

Dovi just shrugs his shoulders apologetically as Sol looks at him after my car story.

"If you would've seen what car he chose for us, you'd believe it!" Dovi says bursting into a laugh. "I just couldn't cram myself into that tiny little box for three weeks."

Dovi turns the tables on him and starts questioning Sol.

"So now that you know why we are here, what brings you to Aspen?"

"Well I'm here because there is a bluegrass concert today up this mountain."

"You came in just for this concert?"

"Well, yes."

"So what do you do?"

"Right now I'm just drifting. I travel around and follow different bands I like."

"How do you pay for the tickets?"

"I usually don't pay. I volunteer to help the organizers and get in that way. I actually have to go meet the organizers of this concert very soon. They told me to check in with them a little while before the concert starts and it'll start in an hour or an hour and a half."

"Maybe before you go you want to put on Tefillin?"

"It was nice bumping into you fellows. You both are more interesting than most of the people I usually meet, however I really have to go..."

"It has been extremely nice to have met you. Like I said before, we literally flew thousands of miles to spend some time with you. How about we at least walk you to your meeting place?" Dovi offers with his witty smile.

"No problem man. That would be awesome! I'd like to hang out with you."

As we walk up the mountain to Sol's meeting, we turn more than a few heads. Sol with his hippy clothes that desperately needed to be laundered and his long 'fragrant' dreadlocks, and us, two Chasidic men sporting our formal black and white attire really stuck out in the colorful, posh, Aspen crowd.

As we walk further and further we get to know more and more about Sol. He showered whenever a nice motel or hotel worker would allow him and his friends to use a room to clean themselves. He volunteered for food and no, he didn't travel alone, he had a girlfriend, a non-Jewish girlfriend...

She meets up with us and we exchange brief polite pleasantries. About two minutes later she excuses herself.

Sol confesses to us "You know this girl is really sweet and I really care for her but I have some reasons to believe that she is cheating on me."

"That is just not kosher! This girl is just no good." Dovi strongly protests.

"No. She really is a great girl, she just isn't perfect. That's what's bothering me."

"Not perfect? Listen to yourself. You are justifying a wrong behavior."

Dovi takes the opportunity to talk to our new friend about how Jewish men should only date and marry Jewish ladies. This subject being a very touchy topic amplified with the alarming statistics that fifty percent (or more) of unobservant Jews in America intermarry.

His diplomatic tone of voice, spoken slower with more emphasis for dramatic effect, doesn't water down the conveyed content; yet, he resembles someone walking on eggshells as he proceeds with great caution.

"Didn't your mother or father ever talk to you about how important it is to date a Jewish girl? You know these things lead to something..."

"What can I do? I met this girl and I love her." He admits.

"Well the person you 'love' is really someone else's soul mate."

"Doesn't love mean something?"

"Yes it most definitely means something... It means you're in trouble! You developed feelings for someone who isn't yours!"

"How do you know?"

"I know because a Jew has a Jewish soul whose other half is a Jewish one. A non-Jew has a different soul and they have a different soul mate...A union of a Jew and a non-Jew is just a soul mismatch. If you really love this girl you'd want her to find her own soul mate instead of being selfish and hold onto something that isn't yours and keeping your very own soul mate waiting... "

"I don't know man." Sol says.

"Just because you don't know doesn't mean the subject is in the gray zone...Your soul mate is waiting for you and she is a wonderful Jewish girl."

"I appreciate your honesty, but let me also be honest, I'm not an observant Jew. I'm not religious..."

"It doesn't matter if you're religious or observant or not when it comes to who you are. You are one hundred percent Jewish just like me. There's no fifty percent or a twenty percent Jew. If your mother is Jewish, you are one hundred percent Jewish! Just because you haven't had the privilege to learn much of the treasures within the Torah and Judaism doesn't mean that it isn't yours just as it is mine. By the way, that's what I'm here for, to remind you about your great inheritance..."

"Thank you so much. Therefore what?"

"Therefore you should date only Jewish girls because, G-d willing, that will lead to marrying a Jewish girl and having a Jewish family..."

"Wow, family? I'm not even thinking about that yet. I just want to have a good relationship."

"Listen, you should start thinking about these things. A relationship is serious business."

"This subject is heavy."

"Yes it is. You should know, whether your parents told you or not, Jews date and marry Jews, only!"

"Come on, it's too hard..."

"If I can do it, you can do it..."

Sol's face takes on a pensive expression as he contemplates the verbal exchange as we walk up the mountain. It appears to be touching a raw nerve.

As we finally arrive at the entrance of the large tented concert area, situated on a large plateau a third of the way up the mountain, we are confronted with an awkward feeling of separation. We have been conversing for what seems like a long time.

Not knowing if we will get another chance, I ask enthusiastically again "Sol before you go, would you like to perform the great Mitzvah of putting on Tefillin?"

"I'm sorry, but I really can't right now. I've been trying unusually hard to get in to this concert. It's a top priority for me. This band is one of my all-time favorites. I can't be late to meet with the concert crew. However, if they have enough help and they do not need me, I'll do whatever Mitzvah you like."

"It's our paramount priority for you to perform this Mitzvah, so we'll wait for you here. Just in case..."

With those parting words, Sol disappears into the concert grounds via the service entrance for his meeting.

"What are the chances to have met a drifting youth like this in glitzy Aspen, of all places, under these circumstances? Meeting him is nothing short of a miracle! We must Daven that he doesn't get in!" Dovi declares.

"I can't believe how close he is, yet so far away! If only Hashem gives us another opportunity..." I lament.

Next to the trees, on the side of the mountain, under an immense blue sky, we sound our sincere pleas and prayers that we will get another chance to merit Sol's soul. It would be great to talk with him some more, and help him perform this very holy deed.

Our heartfelt supplications seem to have ascended 'up the mountain' almost immediately.

Shortly after we parted, we see Sol returning to us sporting a dejected face.

"This never happens to me! I always get in." Sol complains when he reaches us. He is terribly sad over the fact that he will not be going into the concert.

"This is called Hashgacha Pratis! Divine providence! You are meant to do a Mitzvah," Dovi states confidently.

"I guess you're right..." Sol mumbles as he lowers his head and looks at the ground. "Maybe we can go down the mountain. There are tables and benches down there," he suggests.

"No problem. Let's go..." I say.

We descend from the plateau and head towards the table area down below.

It happens to be on a very busy, central point on the path where people go up and down the mountain.

When we reach it, I'm surprised by the sheer amount of people passing through.

I place my Tefillin bag on the table and face him.

"Sol, we are going to do a very holy Mitzvah. The word Mitzvah is a very famous word. Everybody has some understanding of it; however I want to add to that which you know with something you might not know."

Sol's reddish brown eyes lock onto mine in concentration.

"The word Mitzvah literally means a commandment. A certain act commanded by G-d. Interestingly, in Aramaic the word Mitzvah means connection. So essentially by performing a Mitzvah we connect to His very will. That is true with every Mitzvah, but this really manifests in quite a literal way with Tefillin. We bind these two boxes with these leather straps to our body. They contain holy verses inscribed on parchment. One box is placed on the left bicep facing one's heart and its strap is bound around our arm. This represents subjugating one's heart to G-d. The box placed above the forehead held in place by its own strap represents subjugating one's mind to G-d. Jewish men are commanded to connect to the Creator in this manner every day except for Shabbos and holidays. This act is very, very, special. "

"What an introduction!" Sol exclaims thankfully.

"It makes a difference to learn a little about something before doing it, don't you agree? Are you ready?" I ask as I take the arm Tefillin out of the bag.

"I don't know what to do." He admits bashfully.

"Don't worry. I'll help you along. We will say the blessing on the Tefillin at the beginning of the wrap. Don't speak until I place the head Tefillin on you. Ok?"

Sol nods his head in agreement.

"Are you a righty or a lefty?"

"I'm a righty."

"OK. Now roll up the sleeve of your left arm. Take off your watch. The Tefillin must be directly on your skin without any separation. Just like we should let nothing separate us from G-d…"

I place the arm Tefillin on his bicep and say the blessing with him word for word. I proceed to wrap the leather strap around his arm and then I secure the head Tefillin above his forehead between his eyes with the two straps dangling down his chest one on either side.

The regular looks we have been getting turn to stares and double takes from the random passersby.

I open the Siddur, the prayer book, and offer it to him.

"Do you need help reading the Hebrew or should I say it with you?"

"Could you read it with me?"

"Sure."

We read the 'Shema Israel' prayer together. I say a word and he repeats it after me. Sol's eyes turn soulful as he looks at the words on the pages I'm reading from. The energy of the moment is intense, and somehow transforms into becoming very personal.

Then all of a sudden while Sol is still wearing the Tefillin on his head and arm, we are approached by a stranger. The man directs his attention to me and looks me in the eye.

"Excuse me Rabbi. I happen to have this ticket to the blue grass concert starting soon up the mountain. I won't be able to make it, something came up. Would you like the ticket?" He held the ticket in his hand moving it suggestively towards me.

Sol is amazed, Dovi is taken aback, and I am very surprised by this 'coincidental' gift offering.

"I'm not going to be able to go to the concert, however, I have a friend who would love to get into this concert. " I say with a smile as I look at Sol who is looking on with his mouth open.

The man hands me the ticket and disappears as quickly as he appeared. I hand Sol the ticket into the hand that still has the Tefillin on it.

"I can't believe this!" He gasps looking at his arm wrapped with the straps then looking at the ticket he is holding with that arm's hand.

"This is unreal!"

"You see, you just did a Mitzvah and Hashem gave you a little sign. This doesn't happen every day you know…" Dovi says.

Sol is visibly affected by the fact he 'miraculously' received a ticket for the concert he has tried to get into so desperately, without any success, until right after he put on Tefillin.

"Don't think that by doing Mitzvos you get what you want. The gift itself is fulfilling the desire of the Creator, by performing His Mitzvos and studying His Torah..." I add.

"Whatever you say man, but this is really trippy..." he concludes shaking his head.

I remove the Tefillin from Sol's head and arm and wrap the straps around the boxes before putting them in their velvet bag.

"Sol we have to go. We have to continue on our trip. We are headed to Vail next."

"It was really nice hanging out with you guys. Let me walk you to your car."

"That would be very nice of you."

The three of us are walking against the current of people coming up to the concert on the mountain as we head down the road to the parking area.

We speak further making small talk. After a little pause in our conversation Sol confesses to us...

"I was thinking about it, and I've come to the conclusion I will give my ticket to my girlfriend. She'll go in instead of me."

"Sol, what are you saying? After all this you are just going to give it away to this girl who is cheating on you?" Dovi asks in disbelief.

"Sol, I gave the ticket to you. Not to her." I protest.

"I know, I just don't feel good about going myself since we came in together to go to the concert. It would be rather selfish and rude, no?"

We answer Sol with our silence. His etiquette and sensitivity are right on.

We step closer to the direction of our car where out of the blue a man walks over to me from the side and stops me in my tracks with a smile.

"Hello! How are you today rabbi?" He greets me.

"Thank G-d, very well." I answer back.

"Listen, I bought a ticket for the concert up there. Something came up and I will not be able to go, would you like to go instead of me?" He offers.

Sol's eyes immediately widen while his jaw literally drops in awe as he hears this.

I myself am quite stunned as I answer, "I will not be able to go to the concert, but my friend here would love to go..."

The man gives me the ticket and vanishes into the crowd. I turn my face to Sol and hand him the second ticket.

"This is a miracle! Are you guys' angels or something?" He asks incredulously.

"No, just rabbis in training..." I answer wearing a vague smile.

"Isn't it amazing that just after you told us you'll be giving the first ticket away, someone just gives me a second ticket?! I hope you don't take this to mean you two should enjoy the concert together..." I give Sol a knowing look.

"Don't worry; she'll be hanging out with her friends anyway." Sol reassured me. "But, I am so grateful to be able to go to the concert too. Thank you so much."

"First of all, I will worry until you find a good Jewish girlfriend. Second, don't thank us, thank G-d!" Dovi declares.

The crowd around us is hurrying to the concert which will commence shortly. We get to the parking area and he is still with us.

"It was really special meeting you!" Sol says as he wraps his arms around Dovi in a bear hug.

"Meeting you made our day." Dovi says.

Sol then gives me a big hug and says" I'm not going to thank you for the tickets. I'll thank G-d..."

"Goodbye." Sol says with a melancholy hint of sadness.

"Chasidim don't say goodbye. We hope to see each other again..."I say. "I wish we could stay in touch."

"Well that's going to be a little hard since I'm travelling around. I don't know where I'll go next. I don't have a phone and I don't have an e mail account."

I reach into my pocket and produce a Chabad Lubavitch business card. I hand it to him.

"What's this" he asks.

"Wherever you might roam, you can always come home. It's a card with a general number to call wherever you are to connect you with a local Shliach, a Chabad rabbi. You are always welcome, anywhere." I positively say.

In addition, I hand him some authentic Jewish inspirational reading material to keep.

He stands a few feet away, in the current of people, looking at us with those big reddish brown eyes.

It seems that our new friend is sad to see us go.

We head to our car and I look back a couple of times to see him lingering there, with the mountain behind him, staring at us. Each time I wave he waves back.

We get into our car and slowly drive away.

I look back and he is still there following us with those eyes, holding the two tickets, his two miracles, close to his heart.

୫୦୯୨

The sun on our flight is shining with an unusual golden light as we ascend into the skies, transcending the earth and the clouds below.

I get a flashback of the cliff side road to Aspen when we were literally driving above the clouds.

Here we are, two rabbinic students who spent eighteen days on these spiritual soul travels that spanned some 2,600 miles through Colorado and Wyoming. Now, we are going back to our New York home.

I look out of the window and let the sun's rays warm my face as I reflect on some highlights of our recent ventures.

The mysterious chain of acquaintances that lead us to a recluse living on the outskirts of Nederland in the woods...

The emotionally charged meeting with a convicted family man who we visited in his Cheyenne prison, through the efforts of the Aleph Institute...

How we drove 13 long hours to meet with 'just' one Jew living in Jackson Hole.

The guru hunt we were given, attempting to make contact with an elusive celebrity 'spiritualist' who happened to be a Cohen, and his angry non-Jewish wife who was outraged that we found them.

The intriguing phone call and hospital visit to an ex-Lubavitcher who formed his own reformed sect in Boulder.

The grueling call-a-thon and challenging house calls from the lists of Jews we were given to contact.

The unnerving encounter with the man in Denver whose drugs sadly debilitated him.

And off course...our 'coincidentally random' meeting with Sol.

As I meditate on our long drives through the vast open spaces and the holy souls we met, I marvel at this extremely unique experience we were privy to.

I can't help but think that this whole trip was reminiscent of those stories I read of the Baal Shem Tov and his Chasidim travelling around reaching out to fellow Jews amidst much revealed divine providence and miracles so many years ago.

If I let myself dare to compare, I really feel this truly was a modern day Baal Shem Tov-type road trip!

As I study the different shapes of the clouds underneath, different memories form within me. The image of the young man we met in Denver, who was on drugs and nodded off while I put Tefillin on him, comes to the forefront of my mind.

I let my thoughts wander…

This man could very well be symbolic of many assimilated Jews, I contemplate to myself. Like drugs, common culture intoxicates and alters one's consciousness, leaving the people it entertains and occupies under its severe influence. Even when something real, full of meaning and connection come up, the person could be so 'high', he can barely experience it without, 'nodding off' since the poison he has ingested is so potent. Alternatively, I think that the scenario could also be a representational example of not being present fully when engaged in something holy or otherwise important, distracted by foreign thoughts or insignificant preoccupations.

When will he escape the poison prison of bad habits instead of escaping into it?

When will he clean up his act and 'wake up' both physically and spiritually? I wonder.

When will he overcome the polluting distractions and barriers so he will be able to do more of the right thing?

My thoughts change form and reshape, playing back more of our quest. Then the interaction with Sol takes center stage of my undivided concentration.

The image of him standing there, watching us go, flashes before me. I envision Sol amongst the roaring sea of people following us with the windows of his soul wide open.

What will become of him? I wonder.

Maybe he will find his real soul mate, a Jewess, there in the bluegrass mountain concert.

Wouldn't it be great if this nice Jewish boy fulfills his ultimate destiny and settle down and build a warm Jewish family someday, instead of wasting his time or making a grave mistake?

Wouldn't it be amazing if instead of squandering his time drifting to and fro chasing entertainment he will spend it wisely by exploring the depths of the Torah and apply its truth to his every day?

My ponderings halt. I gently scoff and shake my head in disagreement.

Dovi sitting next to me notices and asks "What's on your mind?"

"I'm just thinking about Sol. Remember how he thought that the miracle was getting into the concert with those tickets people gave me?"

"Yes, of course. It was a clear miracle, in fact, two miracles." Dovi answers.

"Well. I was thinking about it and I disagree! The miracle wasn't getting the tickets so he can do what he thinks he wants. The miracle was meeting him and enabling him to do what his soul truly desires, to do what G-d wants of him..."

The sun is brightly casting a truly energized magnificent light unlike I've ever seen.

Could this be a sign of satisfaction with our work from up above?

Internally too, these eighteen days ignite in me an especially lively fire. A hidden switch has been turned on.

I secretly vow to not forget what I experienced and learned on this adventure.

I wish to continue being a catalyst for connecting my fellow Jews to our Creator.

Whatever happens in the future, if I'll be an official rabbi or not, I know this Baal Shem Tov trip is never ending.

I must keep this distinct vibrant light illuminating forever.

೮ාଓ

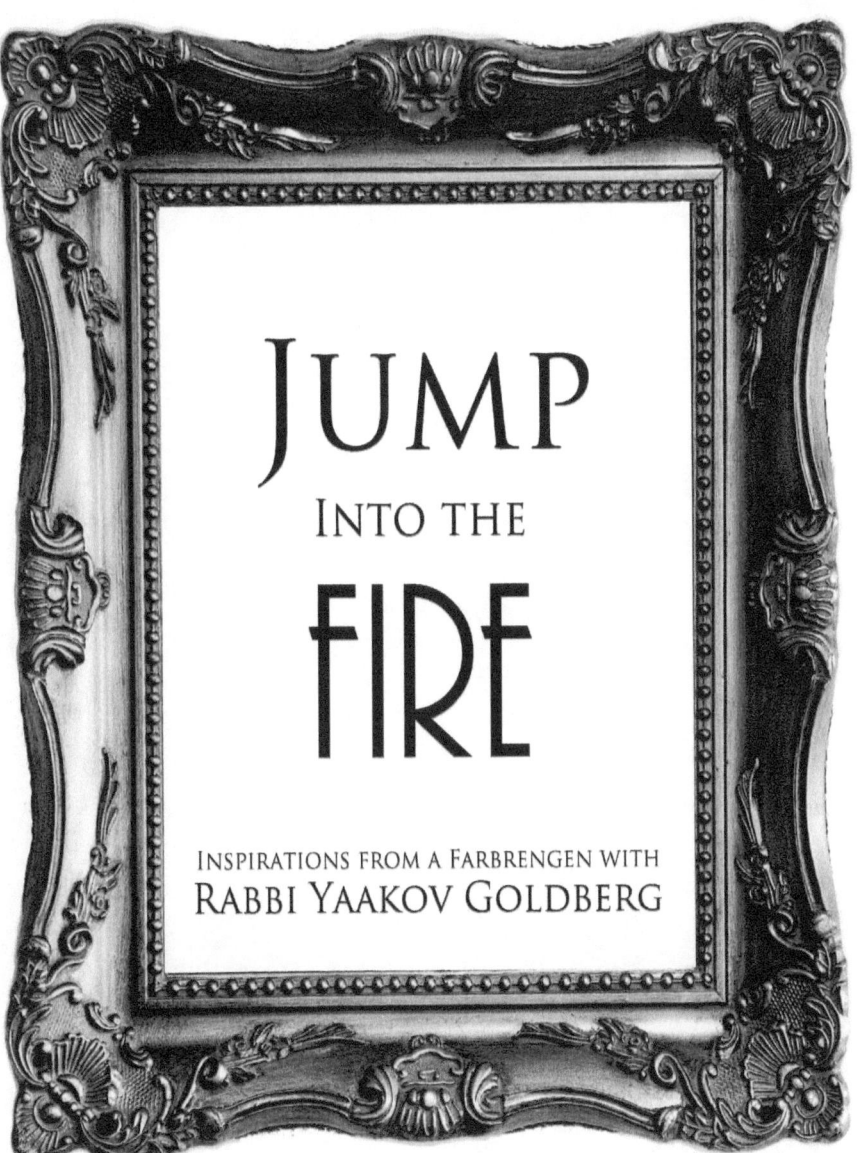

JUMP
INTO THE
FIRE

INSPIRATIONS FROM A FARBRENGEN WITH
RABBI YAAKOV GOLDBERG

"I was asked to speak about my father (the famed scholar **Rabbi Yosef Goldberg***, the Rosh Yeshiva of the Tomchei Tmimim Yeshiva in Brunoy, France), so let me tell you a few stories..."*

YOUNG HEROES

Chaim Tashkenter, a long time resident of Crown Heights, was a friend of my father's. Once, he related to me that he saw my father in his youth in Russia, outside on the street one time, with his head all bandaged up. Shocked and horrified at the sight of his dear friend in such an awful predicament, he immediately approached him and asked what happened.

My father calmed down R' Chaim and explained that he was really all right. He was just trying to cover up and disguise his beard on his Shlichus travels. He was tired of getting stopped and arrested. Sporting a beard in Russia at the time was irregular and aroused negative attention. Perhaps the individual belongs to a group of people that is counter-revolutionary...

One of the times my father was casually arrested, before he bandaged up his face to cover up his beard, which he never dared cut or trim, he confronted the officers that detained him.

"Why are you arresting me? I'm just a regular citizen who has done nothing wrong."

The officer's reply was that he was arrested simply because he had a beard.

"You look suspicious..."

As a Bochur, from the age of twenty two to the age of twenty-six, my father was a Shliach, an emissary, of the Frierdiker (previous) Rebbe, Rabbi Yosef Yitzchak (Joseph Isaac) Schneersohn, also known as the Rebbe Rayatz.

Most of the Shluchim that were employed by the Frierdiker Rebbe at the time were Bochurim, unmarried Yeshivah students..

The reason for this was simple. A married Chasid who was caught and killed would leave behind a widow and orphans; on the other hand a Bochur is just a single individual and therefore not such a big sacrifice if he were to be killed.

What would those Bochurim do? They would travel all over the Soviet Union starting up Chadarim, Jewish schools for children.

The process was that first they would go to the Shamash of the Shul and ask permission to use a corner of the Shul to teach Torah to Jewish kids. Then they would try to gather students.

The number of students was irrelevant. Even a couple of children or even one child would be enough of an enrollment to call the new 'institution' a Cheder, a school of Jewish studies.

Every Neshamah, soul, counted and was of utmost importance.

Some Chadarim had ten kids, some twenty, some just two.

The Bochur who had gathered them together would do whatever was necessary to keep his Cheder in operation.

Sometimes he would teach, sometimes he would fundraise, and whenever possible he would also recruit new students. He was devoted to doing whatever the job demanded in order to keep those Jewish kids learning Torah.

The intensity with which the Frierdiker Rebbe operated can be illustrated by the following story. At the Purim Farbrengen in 1927 which lead to his most famous arrest, the Frierdiker Rebbe asked a Chosid of his what would he do if he would be asked by the KGB to make the following choice, "If you will send your child to a Jewish Cheder we will throw you in the fire. If you send them to a regular state school you will be allowed to live."

Without waiting for a reply the Frierdiker Rebbe declared, *"You should jump into the fire to have your child learn in a Jewish school!"*

My father confided in me that as a young man, during those years when he worked as a Bochur Shliach of the Rebbe Rayatz, he would leave his home each morning, unsure if he would return that night.

My father and all of his friends, the other Bochurim who worked tirelessly as Shluchim, never saw the Frierdiker Rebbe, nevertheless, they put their lives on the line to follow his mandates. They believed in him. They had Bittul, nullification, to their Rebbe.

In many ways those days in Soviet Russia parallel our times now where many Chassidim of the younger generation never saw the Rebbe. We may even say that those people who did see the Rebbe, but it isn't recognizable on them that they saw him could also be grouped in that category.

Those Bochurim were willing to go on self-sacrifice and die following the Frierdiker Rebbe's call to enliven Jews with Torah and Mitzvos, without even having seen their Rebbe once. So too those who haven't seen our Rebbe can follow his teachings and go on self-sacrifice to live and enliven others following the Rebbe's directives and be all that the Rebbe wanted from us to be as Chasidim, and as Yidden.

SPIRITUAL MESSAGES

When France was facing the mounting pressure of the upcoming invasion by the approaching Nazi army, R' Leibish Heber was contemplating his future.

Should he remain in France where he had a well-established, booming business, or should he use his connections and flee to America where he had nothing?

After weighing and contemplating both options in his mind, it seemed to him that the more logical route would be to stay in France, since he was well established and successful there.

He spoke to the Rebbe, who also lived in France at the time, about his great dilemma. The Rebbe told him that since he is a Chasid he should contact his Rebbe, the Rebbe Rayatz. The Chasid was baffled at the idea since the Frierdiker Rebbe who was in Riga (or Utvosk) at the time was seemingly beyond reach.

"How will my question ever reach him?" he asked. The idea seemed futile.

The Rebbe told him that all he has to do was send the Frierdiker Rebbe a letter and he will find a way to answer him. At the Rebbe's insistence, he went to Western Union to deliver a telegram to Riga.

When he asked the workers there for help he was mocked for his efforts.

During that time of raging war, his telegraph was completely useless, they declared. The Chasid insisted on sending the telegram, which they did.

The very next morning, the Chasid awoke with a feeling of urgency, compelling him to flee and make use of his contacts to escape to America, despite his initial thoughts and leanings towards staying in France.

He knew he had gotten his answer from the Rebbe Rayatz. His Rebbe had answered him.

He fled and his life was saved.

Various Chasidim facing many different dire straits who could not establish an ordinary correspondence with the Rebbe Rayatz, sent messages to the Rebbe, along with their requests, by imagining the Rebbe's picture in their minds.

The Rebbe would receive these messages, and the Rebbe found a way to answer them. These answers weren't in letter format, but were dressed in a feeling, clarity in the matter, or a sequence of events that resolved all doubts.

People now may also be baffled or unsure, and wonder how they will get answers from the Rebbe now that they can't see him. Now too, an individual can get an answer. You just send your letter, or imagine the Rebbe's image in your mind and send a message and the answer will come.

The Rebbe will find a way to answer...

SOMETHING INSTEAD OF NOTHING

My father was born to a Chasidic family that was not Lubavitch. They were Chortkov Chasidim, a Chasidus which was founded by one of the Ruzhiner Rebbe's children.

He was orphaned from his father at the age of three and a half. His mother was left with the responsibility of supporting her five children, the oldest of which was fifteen at the time. She had four girls and one son, her youngest, my father.

Since there was no welfare system in Russia, she was forced to find work to feed her family. Unable to find employment, she began making Mashke, alcoholic beverages, and selling them. Then in Russia, this activity was illegal and she was arrested a number of times. She was forced, by her circumstances, to work with great self-sacrifice to support her growing children.

The communist regime brainwashed my father's sisters, whose minds became poisoned by the local schools. They 'left Yiddishkeit' regardless of what their mother said or tried to do. Seeing the destructive effects the local secular schools had on her daughters, she vowed not to let her son, Kadishel, succumb to this G-dless system. She called him Kadishel because he was her only son, the only one who will say Kadish for her after she passes on....

His mother kept him home for years, practically doing nothing much of the time. The little amount of learning he did was with the local Rabbi who taught him together with his own son by his mother's request.

He wasn't only clever, but he was a brave boy as well. Once when he was riding a train someone was mocking him about his Jewish clothing. When the conductor of the train approached, he got his attention and asked him, "Mr. Conductor isn't it the law that dogs must have a muzzle over their mouths when they ride the train?"

"Yes, it's true." The conductor replied.

"Then how come he isn't wearing a muzzle?" My father asked, pointing at the person harassing him. Back then in Russia calling someone a dog was a very serious thing.

When my father reached the age of thirteen, a Jew who happened to be traveling through town started up a conversation with him. He was impressed with the young boy's sharp mind and he told him that a boy such as him ought to be studying in Yeshivah. It would be such a pity to waste such a brain...

The man's words found their way into his heart and he started pestering his mother to send him to

Yeshivah. Being on the thin side, she said she would only send him if he promised to gain some weight. He tried gaining weight, and when the time for him to get measured and weighed finally came, he added a few rocks to his pockets just to help tip the scales, which they did...

The local Rabbi suggested they apply to the Yeshivahs in the city of Kremanchuk. The city of Kremanchuk had two Yeshivahs, one Lubavitch and the other one was Litvish. As per the Rabbi's advice, they sent letters to both Yeshivahs, impatiently waiting for a reply. The first Yeshiva to reply was the Lubavitch Yeshivah, to which he eagerly decided to attend. Years later he would reflect on this and say 'Oh, what would have happened if the other Yeshivah would have sent their letter of acceptance first, what would have been with me then?'

(Somebody in the crowd loudly remarked "You would be in Lakewood now!"

Sharply, Rabbi Goldberg replied, "Those people in that Litvish Yeshiva never made it to Lakewood...!")

Who was that man who planted the idea in my father's head to go to Yeshiva? My father didn't know. He was simply heaven sent!

The last year of my father's life he lived in our house. At that point he was already an aged man and was physically suffering. He lived in my study where we also had an oxygen tank to help him breath.

One time many of his kids and grandchildren were there. Gazing at the many faces all around he remarked how fortunate he was to have gone to the Lubavitch Yeshivah in his youth.

He recounted how his sisters used to tease and torment him while he pursued Yeshivah learning. Once they even cut off his Peyos! He recalled their antagonizing words from so many years ago, "What will become of you? Absolutely nothing! You are not only risking your life, you are completely wasting it with these Jewish studies. The direction your life is taking renders it practically worthless!"

In contrast to my father's life of learning and teaching Torah while nurturing his large observant Jewish family, what at the end became of his anti-religious sisters? Ironically, and sadly enough, their lives amounted to not much more than nothing...

He recognized how sticking with the Rebbe was good for him materially, and of course, spiritually.

By now, my father has literally hundreds of descendants, may they increase in number and be blessed.

A TALE OF TWO VESSELS

There is a striking Midrash that details the following story. There was a poor woman who was drawing water by a well with her earthenware pitcher. Somehow the pitcher fell into the well, out of her reach. The poor lady tried again and again to retrieve her utensil to get water for herself and her family, but it was all to no avail. She started asking passersby to help her. Nobody wanted to help her fetch such an inexpensive vessel.

A while later a king's daughter came with a beautiful gold pitcher with which to draw water from the well. Her golden vessel fell, and immediately she got someone to help her regain it. Before the helper involved himself with saving the precious golden pitcher, the poor woman asked him to get her pitcher too. True, it was inexpensive, but to her it was invaluable.

This story is brought by the Midrash to illustrate a special relationship between Moshe Rabbeino and the Yidden, his flock. Even though Moshe desperately desired to ascend to the Land of Israel, Hashem told him it wasn't fitting to abandon his people in the desert. The most appropriate thing was to stay in the desert and help them. When the Geula takes place and we will experience Techias Hamesim, the revival of the dead, when it's time for Hashem to revive Moshe, Moshe will help the Yidden come back to life as well.

As holy and coveted as it is to be buried in Israel, the Chabad Rebbeim are nevertheless buried outside of the Holy Land. This Midrash can help us understand why. They are buried outside of Israel to help all the Jews who are living outside of Israel until the coming of Mashiach in the Geula Hashleima, the complete redemption.

NOT I !

The Alter Rebbe was distraught over the fact he couldn't understand something his Rebbe, the Maggid of Mezeritch, had given over and taught his students. As much as he tried to figure it out, thinking and rethinking about the topic, his question remained unsolved. He decided he must go to the Maggid's home and ask him personally.

He knocked on the Maggid's door and the Maggid asked, "Who is it?"

"It is I," the Alter Rebbe answered.

The Maggid didn't open the door and again he asked, "Who is it?"

"It's me," the Alter answered again. "It is I".

The Maggid opened the door and answered the question after which he asked the Alter Rebbe to do him a favor.

"There is a Bris in a nearby town which I wanted to attend but I will be unable to go. Could you go and represent me and be my Shliach?"

The Alter Rebbe agreed.

"You don't have to reveal who you are," the Maggid suggested. "Just be there and that is enough…"

The Alter Rebbe went to the Bris which took place in the home of the father of the baby boy who happened to be a very wealthy man. Everything went fine; however, as people were leaving the maid noticed that one of the expensive silver spoons was missing.

Immediately the suspicion fell on the stranger there, the Alter Rebbe.

"Did you take the spoon?" they asked him.

"No it wasn't me," he replied.

They didn't relent and their accusations grew stronger, "You took the spoon didn't you? Just confess!"

"No. It wasn't I," the Alter Rebbe innocently exclaimed.

They took the Alter Rebbe and they started beating him screaming, "Confess you were the one who took the spoon. Thief, confess!"

The Alter Rebbe cried out again and again as they hit him, "It's not I. It's not me."

Suddenly, after a while, the maid called out from the kitchen "Stop. I found the spoon. It was stuck to another spoon. I found it. It was a mistake!"

Upon returning to the Maggid, the Alter Rebbe told him he went to the Bris and related what happened there. However he had a small question…

"I did your Shlichus. I went to the Bris but why did I have to go through the humiliation of being called a thief and being beaten?"

The Maggid answered him, "When you came to me before, you knocked on my door and I asked 'Who is it?' you answered, 'It is I', and 'It's me'. There was a sense of Yeshus, ego, and of feeling of oneself, in your answer, 'It is I' that had to be rectified…"

This generation is the Gilgul, a reincarnation, of the Dor HaDe'ah, the generation of the Jews who left Egypt and died in the desert. Dor De'ah means the generation of knowledge, since these people had an intimate knowledge of Hashem. They were taken out of Egypt, saw the splitting of the Red Sea, received the Torah and saw many miracles for 40 years as they traveled through the desert.

As we are getting closer to Mashiach and the Geula there's an explosion of De'ah, knowledge. However there is De'ahs Havaya, knowledge of G-dliness, and LeHavdil, in direct contrast, De'ahs Shtos, knowledge of nonsense.

De'ah also means opinion. This generation everybody has an opinion. Even a young child has an opinion. A ninety five year old could be teaching a five year old something and the five year old says, 'This is your

JUMP INTO THE FIRE

opinion. It could be good for you, but I have a different opinion.'

This generation's Tikkun, rectification, is the Bittul, nullification, of the 'I'.

Practically, a Chasid does this by being Mevutal, nullified, to the Rebbe, which means that in every situation and step in life he or she does what the Rebbe had instructed.

(Someone from the crowd asked, "But Rabbi Goldberg, doesn't it say in our Torah that one should learn whatever is comfortable to him? There is a place in Torah for Yeshus, ego."

To which Rabbi Goldberg responded "That's not what it says. It says 'SheYilmud BeMakom Shelibo Chafetz'. A person should learn a subject in Torah that they want, not with what they are comfortable with. Chassidus brings various explanations regarding the difference between Ratzon and Chafetz. Ratzon is the external aspect of desire. Chafetz is the inner aspect of desire. The Torah subjects a person chooses to learn are connected to the individual's very essence. In general, though, the inner desire of every Yid is to cleave to Hashem, to be Buttel, nullified, to Hashem and fulfill his desire. For that, we need the Rebbe to help us.")

I'm not so old but I remember that when I was a child if the parent said something you obeyed. There was no why and no question. It was obvious that the parent loved the child and wanted the very best for them. Now everyone has an opinion.

We must remember 'I' doesn't exist. Only Hashem exists!

RETURN TO SPLENDOR

Hadar Hatorah, the world's first Baal Teshuvah Yeshivah (HadarHatorah.Org, a Lubavitch Yeshivah for Jewish men with little or no formal background in Jewish knowledge or practice) is celebrating teaching for 49 years. Nevertheless, it's here for the sad and regrettable reason that many Jews didn't get a proper Jewish education. It wasn't always like this. People used to keep tradition. There are some people here in this crowd whose grandfathers were religious, but something happened along the way, and their parents just didn't keep it up.

Somehow, because of the hardships this century has brought, we find ourselves in this unfortunate situation which Chabad has been trying to fix.

When he first started learning Gemara, my son Mendy came home from Yeshivah and told me what he had learned. The Yeshivahs classically begin teaching the students the Chapter of 'Elo Metzios' in Gemara Bava Metzia.

This chapter deals with the obligation to return a lost object to its owner.

In the beginning of that Gemara, the word 'Hadar' describes a person returning to collect wheat kernels that have fallen and spread. Hadar in Aramaic means to return.

My son then explained to me his interpretation of the meaning of words 'Hadar Hatorah'.

He told me, "The name Hadar Hatorah means 'Return to Torah' and it's all about returning Jews back to the authentic Torah way."

(In Hebrew, Hadar means splendor or beauty; therefore literally, 'Hadar Hatorah' means 'the splendor/beauty of Torah.')

NOTHING STANDS BEFORE A PERSON'S DESIRE!

R' Yekusiel Lepler, who was a Chasid of the Alter Rebbe, was a salt merchant by trade. He lived in the city of Lipali. He was one of the known Ovdim (workers), Chasidim who used to work on the refinement of their character and Daven, pray, for hours. Even though he was an Oved, his Torah knowledge in general, and Chassidus in particular, was minuscule and very limited, to say the least...

One time, a young Chasid of the Mittler Rebbe passed through Lipali and stayed there for a week. Every day he used to teach a Ma'amar, a Chassidic discourse of the Mittler Rebbe, in which extremely deep concepts were expounded upon and explained. Being that this young Chasid was a great scholar and an excellent speaker, he impressed all of his listeners.

The Chasid R' Yekusiel, who wasn't mentally gifted, didn't understand these complex Ma'amarim, which effected his self-esteem greatly. He felt depressed and low because of it to the extent he internally criticized and chastised himself with humiliating names.

Here he was, a forty year old man, who went to the Alter Rebbe for so many years, during which he had learned as much as he could, and here comes this youngster whom he couldn't understand at all!

Every day when he used to hear the young Chasid teach a Ma'amar publicly he felt worse and worse about himself. He even asked the young Chasid to review the Ma'amarim with him privately, repeatedly; however, although he sensed the great loftiness of the concepts, seemingly, every word was beyond his mind's reach.

Finally, he reached the point where he just couldn't take it anymore. He gave over his store's operation to his family's hands, and spent his time exclusively focused on learning with the young Chasid of the Mittler Rebbe for an entire three weeks.

He learned and reviewed night and day, but he saw no progress. When the Chasid left the town, he felt as hopeless as if he was stranded in the middle of the ocean. He cried, he fasted, but nothing he tried helped at all; so he decided he must go to Lubavitch.

When R' Yekusiel arrived in Lubavitch he met with the Mittler Rebbe in Yechidus, a private audience. In Yechidus, he told the Rebbe that he understood the regular Ma'amarim, but their explanations and the deeper ones, he just couldn't comprehend.

The Mittler Rebbe's response was summed up with the declaration, *"Nothing stands in the way of a person's will!"*

When R' Yekusiel realized that it all was dependent on his willpower, he decided to stay in Lubavitch until he would begin to finally understand. He sent a message to his family in Lipali via some travelers that he will stay in Lubavitch for a while; he stayed for four months.

He toiled with great effort during these months. He would contemplate and meditate on one concept for several hours at a time, and he exerted excruciating effort to review concepts, over and over tens of times, until he felt he had mastered them.

This intense labor gave birth to a new entity. The transformed R' Yekusiel finally became a vessel of deep understanding.

The Mittler Rebbe wrote his Sefarim, books, dedicated to various particular individuals. The Rebbe Maharash once told the Rebbe Rashab that Imrey Bina, one of the deepest books in Chassidus, which the Mittler Rebbe had authored, was specifically written for R' Yekusiel Lepler.

He said that R' Yekusiel used to have the mind of a wooden log, even though he used to go to the Alter Rebbe and had great opportunities for private audiences with him. Only when R' Yekusiel decided to actualize his desire to also understand Chassidus well and vigorously labored with himself to achieve it, did he bring himself to an understanding of the most refined and subtle concepts in Chassidus.

The Rebbe Maharash related that once he had some difficulty in understanding something in Imrey Binah. He went to his father, the Tzemach Tzedek, and posed the question hoping for a clarification.

The Tzemach Tzedek told the Rebbe Maharash about R' Yekusiel, and then he mentioned to him that Imrey Binah was written for him. He instructed the Rebbe Maharash to go and ask R' Yekusiel his question and afterwards to inform him of what he said, then he, the Tzemach Tzedek, will answer him.

When the young Rebbe Maharash approached R' Yekusiel after his long Davening, prayer, R' Yekusiel told him that he is a businessman, and as such he will only sell his merchandise, the answer, for a worthy sum. The Rebbe Maharash asked him what he wanted in return. R' Yekusiel answered that he wanted the Rebbe Maharash to review for him the Tzemach Tzedek's Ma'amer from Shabbos and to explain to him all the concepts in it that he did not yet understand. In addition, R' Yekusiel stipulated, those questions that the Rebbe Maharash would not know the answer for, he should ask his father the Tzemach Tzedek for a clarification.

After the Rebbe Maharash agreed, then R' Yekusiel proceeded to answer his question with such clarity and in such a systematic way that the Rebbe Maharash was completely astounded. He just couldn't believe his ears. How could such wondrously profound explanations in all realms of Kabbalah and Chassidus come out of a man whose knowledge in the revealed aspects of Torah was mediocre at best?

When the Rebbe Maharash repeated R' Yekusiel's answer to his father, the Tzemach Tzedek, he said that R' Yekusiel Lepler was a living example of 'Yagata U'Matzasa,' if you toil you will find. R' Yekusiel toiled a lot and he surely found a lot.

Later that night R' Yekusiel came to the Rebbe Maharash to receive his 'payment'.

While the Rebbe Maharash gave over a Chazara, a review, of the Ma'amer of the Tzemach Tzedek, R' Yekusiel listened with his whole body.

When R' Yekusiel started asking questions on the Ma'amer, most of them the Rebbe Maharash couldn't answer, so he had to ask the Tzemach Tzedek as per their agreement. The Rebbe Maharash remembered the week of those long questions of R' Yekusiel and the answers by the Tzemach Tzedek as a week of great delight.

The Frierdiker Rebbe writes that the stories about R' Yekusiel Lepler he had heard from his father, the Rebbe Rashab, made a lasting impression on him. How R' Yekusiel transformed himself from being a simple 'wooden log' to one of the greatest scholars in Chassidus, simply because he had a strong desire, a will, made a great impact on him to the extent that it influenced his daily conduct.

What if we don't have such a passionate will like R' Yekusiel Lepler? *We too, must create that kind of a desire within ourselves!*

SILVER & GOLD

Once by a Farbrengen, the Mittler Rebbe, saw some Chasidim drowning in their sorrow.

He mentioned to them an interesting meaning on the verse 'Atzabehem Kesef Ve'Zahav' which usually translates to 'Their idols were silver and gold'. His play on words was on 'Atzabehem', which is similar to the word 'Atzvot,' sadness, which resulted in an astute insight. Switching the word's meaning in the verse created instead: 'Their sadness is caused by the silver and gold'.

Those Chasidim were downcast because they were immersed in their concerns about their material matters, to which they gave too much attention. Their interest and focus on the material actually became the source and root of their sadness.

I have never met someone who got depressed improving their observance in Yiddishkeit. I haven't heard of anyone having a nervous breakdown from contemplating Yichuda Eilah and Yichuda Tatah (Kabalistic concepts of the unity of Hashem).

People need and want to have, and live, a *real life*. Having 'fun', 'enjoying oneself' and chasing material things isn't real happiness, it isn't real life. True happiness and real life is Hashem, his Torah and Mitzvos.

'We have nothing but the words of the son of Amram, Moshe'.

It cannot be stressed enough that we must nullify our 'I' and connect to the Rebbe who enables us to attain a connection to true real life.

৪৩৫৪৩

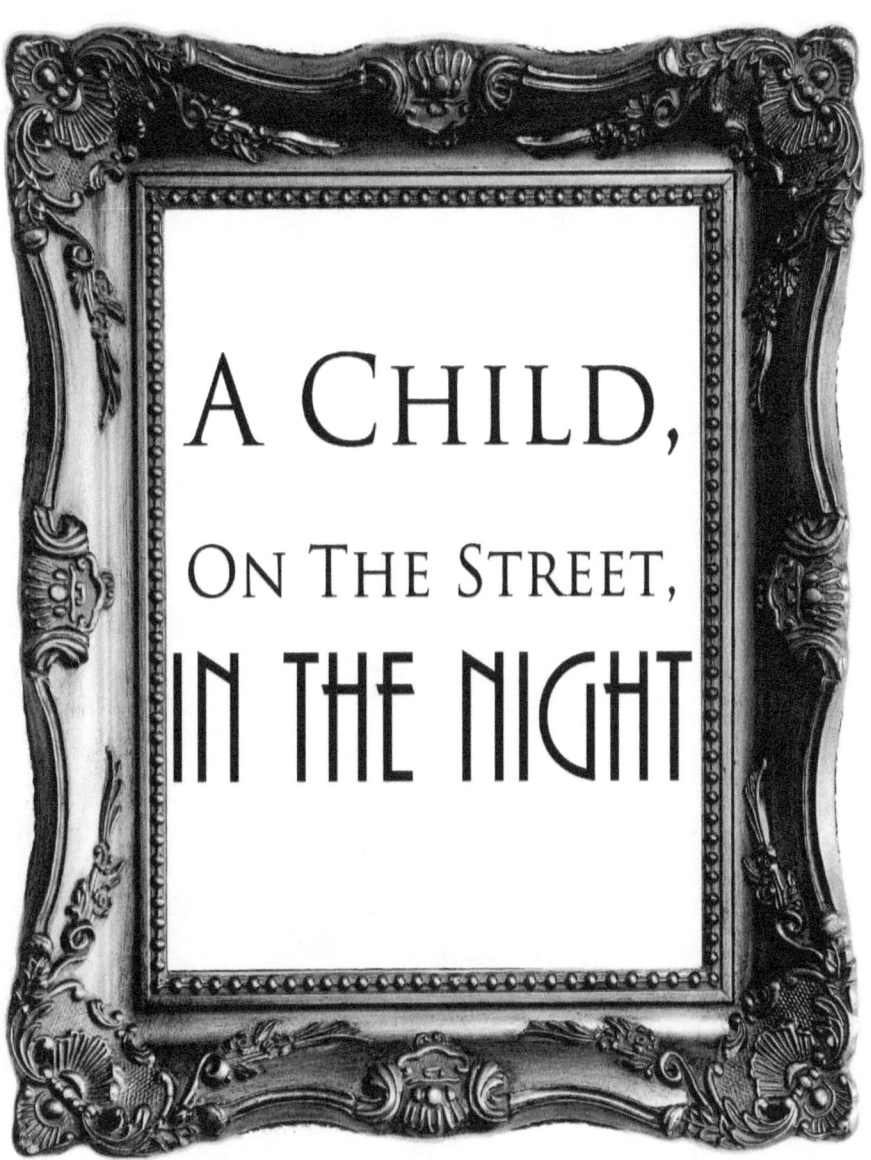

A CHILD,

ON THE STREET,

IN THE NIGHT

ying in bed, fast asleep late Friday night, I hear a man's voice in our Brooklyn apartment. Drifting between sleep and consciousness, I think I'm dreaming. I hope I'm dreaming.

It's just my wife, our kids and me, in our apartment, or so I thought.

But the voice grows stronger, waking me up. I get up and quietly walk towards the noise. Suddenly I hear him again.

"Mr. Klineman, Mr. Klineman..."

Surprisingly, as he calls my name, the unexpected voice doesn't sound threatening at all. Whatever fear I might have had disperses.

"Mr. Klineman, your son..." Hearing my son being mentioned, I hasten my walk to the front door which is wide open.

"Mr. Klineman, your son was outside by the street," the man informs me. He is standing there with my landlord, who is in his pajamas.

"What do you mean ?" I ask him dumbfounded, "Our two year old is sleeping."

"Mr Klineman, your son was outside on the street. He must've opened the doors and gotten out."

I'm completely stunned. "Is he o.k.? Where is he?" I ask, timid of an answer.

"Your son is fine; he is in your apartment already." The nice man reassures me.

I look for my son and see him walking with a bottle, as if nothing happened, in the hallway.

Our baby is fine! Thank you, Hashem!

"How did you find him? What time is it? " I ask, shocked, shaken and physically shaking.

"I'm from Shomrim (Shomrim, guards, are organizations of volunteer civilian patrols which have been set up in many Jewish neighborhoods around the world to combat anti-Semitism and quality-of-life nuisance crimes. They work closely with local police). I was on my patrol and I saw your son by the street on the sidewalk at approximately 4 in the morning. It's after 4am now." He tells me with an expressive face.

My glance drops to the walkie-talkie hanging off his belt.

I had no idea anybody was protecting the neighborhood at such late hours in general, and on Shabbos night in particular. I'm taken aback.

"You might want to double lock your doors from now on." He warns me.

"Your two year old opened all the doors to the outside, be very careful."

"Good Shabbos," he tells me as he goes back outside to continue his patrol.

"Thank you so much. Good Shabbos," I tell both the Shomer and my landlord, who kindly opened our apartment door to the man from Shomrim upon his insistence on waking me up, alerting me to the event that had just transpired.

Apparently he wasn't successful in waking us up by just knocking on the door at this late hour…

ଚ୨ଓଽ

After they left, both my wife and I just cannot stop kissing our beloved little baby boy, afraid to entertain any thought whatsoever as to what could've happened, G-d forbid, in the dark street. We place him on the bed and hug him nonstop.

"We love you." We tell him again and again.

We are utterly unnerved. My heart is pounding.

ଚ୨ଓଽ

As he falls asleep, safe in his bed, we talk about this bizarre circumstance.

"How could this have happened? How could he open all three doors to the outside?" I wonder.

"He was looking for me." My wife states simply. "Around this time of night he always wakes up and comes to my bed. Tonight I fell asleep in the girl's room, and since he didn't see me in my bed, he went searching for me."

"That doesn't make sense. Why would he open the doors and go outside?" I ask.

"Well it kind of happened before. One time I left him in front of the computer to watch a DVD while I went downstairs to get the girls from the school bus. I left the door open just a crack in case he wanted to come down. I guess he got bored of the video and he walked down and saw us just as the girls came from the bus. I opened the door for him downstairs so that he could be outside with us. He probably thought we were downstairs just like last time, however, I had no idea he was capable of opening heavy doors like these. *If I learned one lesson from this it's to never underestimate what a child can do, even a toddler!"*

As I was contemplating my wife's theory, she continued incredulously.

"It's so bizarre, just a couple of days ago a friend of mine was telling me that she made a certain mistake with her kids supervision, and now she looks at her kids with a whole new level of appreciation. She sees Hashem's Hashgacha, G-d's watchfulness, in a revealed way like never before. That friend told me how the toddler of a friend of hers crossed a busy parkway by himself. I immediately judged the mother, thinking how could a mother let such a thing happen, and here something similar just happened to me!"

"I had no idea that someone is patrolling our neighborhood at 4am. Isn't that completely incredible?!" I ask my wife. "What an amazing Hashgacha Pratis, divine providence!" I declare.

"From the entire area of the neighborhood, which is pretty big, for this Shomrim member to just happen to walk by our son and literally save him is extremely extraordinary!"

We are infinitely grateful for the incredible protection that Hashem sent us in the form of an angel from Shomrim, who selflessly was strolling in the wee hours of a Shabbos night while the majority of people in our Brooklyn neighborhood were fast asleep, except for our two year old son!

Thank you, Hashem. Thank you, Shomrim. Thank you, the angel that saved our son.

We can't stop kissing our son this whole Shabbos, and are very appreciative of this special miracle that has just happened to us.

ဆင္စ

In this raw unarmed state of mind, I can't help thinking of how interesting it is that instead of happening on any other Shabbos, or night for that matter, this transpired specifically on this very Shabbos.

This Shabbos is the twelfth anniversary of my first day in Yeshivah.

Growing up, my family kept many Jewish traditions including going to Shul on Shabbos and Yomim Tovim, but we weren't 'religious'. My grandparents were religious, but for whatever reason, it didn't stretch into the next generation.

During my teenage years, we used to go to the Chabad house, which spiritually lifted us to a higher spiritual place, however not until I went to Yeshivah did I actually learn what it really means to be Jewish, something that nobody taught me before.

I went to Hadar Hatorah, when the Yeshivah was in the Catskill Mountains for the summer months.

I was excited about this trip to the country. It was a much needed break from the material madness of New York City's concrete jungle. It seemed like it would be so rejuvenating, so intriguing, learning mysticism in the mountains. It was!

I arrived just as Shabbos was coming in, by a bus and taxi. I placed my bags in the room I was to stay in with the help of a Bochur, a Yeshivah student, and off we went to Shul. When we got to Shul I was impressed by the sheer number of young people in the large room. They were in the middle of singing 'Lecha Dodi', welcoming the Shabbos queen.

My planned two week stay ended up being close to nine years in Yeshivahs and Collels combined.

Now I have a family with children, Baruch Hashem, which all started twelve years ago, that first Shabbos in the Catskill Mountains in Hadar Hatorah.

All those Rabbis along the way, from the Shluchim we met, to the Yeshivah staff, were all my Shomrim, the guards that brought me back home when I was 'on the street, in the night'.

They were there, outside on patrol, looking for Jewish Neshamahs, souls, like mine to remind us that we are outside on the street. They offer a helping hand to bring us back home, ourselves, to 'reunite' with our Jewish identity and Jewish living.

Of course, my parents' desire was the catalyst for all this. They wanted to give their kids a Jewish environment, Jewish experiences and Jewish friends so we would eventually also marry a Jew and live like a Jew. My parents are my special personal Shomrim, since always. They really do get the most credit, for their never-ending support, pushing and encouragement.

༄༅༅

After Shabbos I called the member of Shomrim that brought our son back home. I asked him more detailed questions as to what happened.

"Was he crying when you saw him?" I asked.

"No. He was having a blast." He surprised me with his answer.

"What do you mean?"

"He was playing. He was walking back and forth from the sidewalk to the path by your apartment building."

"Where was he when you saw him?"

"He was by the street, on the sidewalk."

I shudder. Oh, my son!

ဘာ

Naturally the infinite gratefulness I feel towards the Shomer that helped my son extends to the Shomrim that helped me.

Just like my son who was playing outside, on the street in the night unaware of lurking dangers, G-d forbid, I too was playing 'outside, on the street in the night' before my Yeshivah experience.

I was 'playing and having a blast' under the strong influence of 'the world' and popular cultures (with its various guises) in which I was immersed, which demands assimilation to its ideals and common behavior.

Only my Shomrim, the guards of my Jewish soul, my Neshamah, offered another alternative, and suggested quite bluntly, *that there's more to life than this,* much, much more…

৪৩৫৪

Standing there shaking, as the Shomer pulled the rug from under me telling me that my toddler was outside, at four am, I understood like never before, what the Rebbe meant. I understood it on my shivering flesh.

The Rebbe stated again and again via various channels that we cannot just be concerned with our own advancements, be it spiritual or material, while thousands of our brothers and sisters, fellow Jews, are threatened with assimilation and Jewish ignorance, facing spiritual death, G-d forbid.

This time in Jewish history beckons us to literally save Jews, so that they should remain Jewish in the plain sense of the word.

Now, in this day and age, it's actually a matter of Pikuach Nefesh, saving a life, which takes precedence over everything else.

We must reach out to the Jewish people around us, that Jewish child of whatever age, who is playing outside in the dark unaware of any danger to their Jewish identity, and bring them back to their true home, to the Torah and Mitzvahs (commandments).

Even though some Shomrim are official, card carrying ones, *this call of the Rebbe is directed to all of us to become Shomrim*, Jewish guards.

Shomrim who guard all that is Jewish in every Jew, including ourselves, wherever they (we) might be, both in location and level of observance, always reaching higher and higher.

No Neshamah can afford, or deserves to be, underestimated of its potential or denied its spiritual inheritance.

Without my Shomrim, what would have been with me?

෨෨ශ

After all is said and done, all of us, in one way or another, regardless of our knowledge, observance levels and experiences are still just children, outside in the night, this bitter exile.

We are all waiting for our ultimate Shomer, G-d, to come and take us home; the third temple, in the newly built Jerusalem in the expanded Israel; in the complete and final redemption, through his emissary, Mashiach.

May it happen now!

෨෨ශ

andom items appeared missing from our apartment. Could it be due to our sweet hardworking cleaning lady who came highly recommended by neighbors who had used her for the last seven years?

After discussing the matter with our parents, my wife and I concluded it just couldn't be her.... My father-in-law dismissed the idea saying, "Everyone blames the cleaning lady first, and it never is, it's too obvious."

My mother related to us what happened with her one time. My father's passport was missing. Immediately panic set in. They read that passports sometimes are stolen and then sold for much money on the black market.

He had my mother fire their cleaning lady only to find the passport on a shelf a few months later. Oops.

Nevertheless, things *were* missing, including the ring with my grandmother's diamond I gave my wife for our wedding.

We would rationalize that the items were just 'lost' and were going to be found in the near future, which eased our minds.

However, last week, Divine Providence taught us a lesson in trusting 'sweet' strangers.

My mother got our newly pierced-eared girls gold earrings to avoid infection. Designating them as a gift for Shabbos, my wife put them in a cup on a shelf in the kitchen.

The girls would look at the cup on the shelf excited for Shabbos to come, and also when they will wear their grandmother's earrings for the first time. But on Friday, Erev Shabbos, we realized that the earrings were missing.

After asking everyone in the family, we learned that the earrings weren't moved by any one of us.

Funny, the cleaning lady came the day before and all of a sudden the earrings were missing...

Self-doubt set in as we could have unintentionally misplaced them somewhere in the kitchen. After a lengthy search our suspicions were solidified. We then realized that the items were not missing, but rather were stolen, and the cleaning lady had to have done it.

What should we do? A confrontation was necessary.

Since the cleaning lady hardly spoke English, a Spanish speaking friend came to the rescue.

My wife's friend called our cleaning lady and told her that we knew she took things from our home, and that my wife feels very sad about losing the engagement ring and the other items. My wife was willing to give her one chance to return them or else...

The cleaning lady did not confess immediately, but rather exclaimed that she knew where they were and offered to look for the items.

Our Spanish speaking friend suggested we have Miriam S. call her as well. Miriam runs a cleaning service where she screens the ladies thoroughly, and of course, she speaks Spanish.

I don't know what Miriam said, but I know that she did scare our cleaning lady. Instead of coming the next day to clean our apartment and 'show my wife where she put things', the cleaning lady came with her daughter that very evening with a bag full of our jewelry, including the engagement ring!

Her daughter explained that her mother 'found' these around the house when she was cleaning and put them in her pocket. She intended to return them, but she forgot...

More shocked by the miraculous return of many of our precious items that had been stolen, we were shocked that she *really did do it!*

How could this quiet, sweet, hardworking lady to whom we opened our home, betray us?

How could we have sometimes left her in the house by herself?

On occasion, how could we have left her with our babies alone, while getting her money from the bank?

Are we going to get back the other items that were 'missing', that have been taken as well, such as some more jewelry, silverware, the Ipod, some kids shoes and other items we don't even know about?

Meanwhile, we informed our previous neighbor, the one who recommended her 'trustworthy good' cleaning lady to us, of our most current events.

Wowed and scared at the same time, she was dumb struck by the news. She had this cleaning lady for seven years!

Furthermore, she was alarmed at how she routinely left the house with the cleaning lady alone, as well as left her children with her.

Every once in a while when things went missing she wouldn't pay much attention to it, thinking the kids misplaced it. She made a quick list of recent losses: Her daughters China dolls, $100 bill from a guest's suitcase, a $20 bill from her son's room, an Ipod and the list goes on.

Another tough call from Miriam to our 'sweet, good and trustworthy' cleaning lady had her calling us again.

She offered to give us money for the other items. Sifting through various belongings, seemingly from other people, she could no longer find our other possessions.

We were just the tip of the iceberg!

Cleaning provided her with a paid pass into people's homes like ours, whose trust was gained after years of 'good service'. She scouted out the house for valuables to take, the worth of which far outweighed the few dollars an hour she earned by cleaning.

We called a Rov not knowing exactly how much to charge.

We didn't want to steal from our thief...

He told us we can charge her whatever we felt covered the amount since she wasn't telling us exactly what else she took. He also took the opportunity to reprimand us for leaving the cleaning lady in our apartment by herself.

In addition to putting ourselves in danger, he said it could lead to serious problems in Kashrus.

Regarding theft, a common practice among cleaning ladies, I heard about after telling this story to numerous people, is that the cleaning ladies put items they take in the garbage which they take out. Later either they or someone from their family comes around and takes it from the garbage.

The Rebbe teaches us to share what we learned with others.

My family learned a big lesson from our 'sweet, good and trustworthy' cleaning lady. Now we are sharing the lesson we learned with you.

A person easily trusts an individual they see often, like the 'nice and good' cleaning lady. A person might say, "Our cleaning lady is a good one..." but ask yourself, are you absolutely certain that these cleaners' morals are just like yours?

Please protect yourself.

ജാരു

A friend of mine from the Chasidic enclave of Williamsburg (in Brooklyn) shared with me two cleaning lady/nanny horror stories that unfortunately occurred there, G-d forbid.

The first one involved a family who had a woman come to clean and baby-sit their newly born baby so that the mother could go back to work. As time passed they noticed that their baby wasn't behaving normally, something just wasn't right. One time the nanny couldn't come, so the mother stayed home with her children. At one point the baby cried bitterly and wouldn't be appeased regardless of what the mother did. Her seven year old then came to the mother and asked her, why she doesn't do what the nanny /cleaning lady did with the baby to stop the crying.

"What did she do?" The mother asked.

The child took the mother to the kitchen and told her the lady put the baby by the oven and turned the gas on without turning on the fire until the baby fell asleep, aided by the gas fumes!

The second story involves a family who had a lady clean and cook for them for many years. They loved her as if she was part of their family.

After many years had passed, the lady decided that she wanted to retire so she bought a house in her native Poland.

On the day of her departure the family drove their beloved house keeper to the airport.

By the last checkpoint where the family couldn't follow her any further, she stopped and said, "Well now that I'm leaving you are surely going to miss my cooking!"

"Oh yes, we definitely will," the family said warmly.

Smiling she said to them, "You know, whenever I cooked for you I always added a special ingredient with a special flavor, pork, that's why you liked my cooking so much!"

Their close 'family friend' turned around and walked to the plane leaving the Chasidic family completely and utterly stunned.

ುಅ

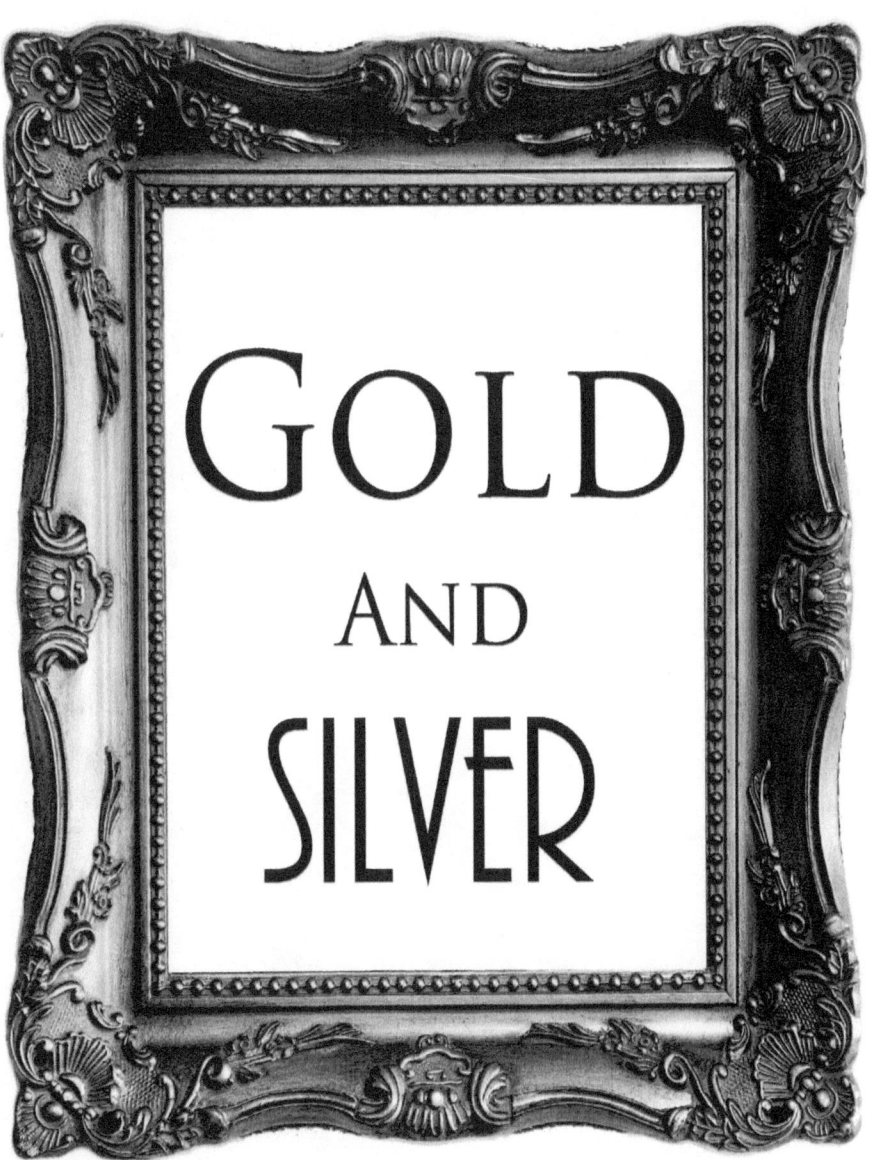

*At Motzei Shabbos Malve Malkas, end of Shabbos gatherings, the **Bobover Rebbe, Rabbi Shlomo Halberstam**, used to share stories and different Torah thoughts with the multitudes of people that came to bask in his light.*

His Gabbai took these opportunities to immortalize his words by scribbling notes from these holy gatherings on the backs of paper plates he took from the tables. A work associate of mine is this Gabbai's grandson. His father has a bunch of these plates with tiny writings that contain the Bobover Rebbe's words. One of the 'dishes' served from the back of one of these plates is the following story...

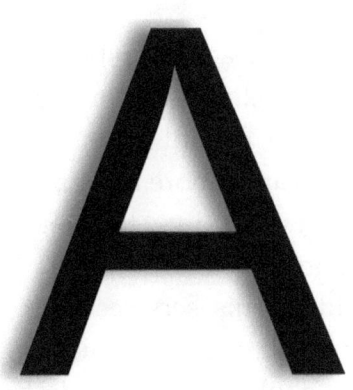

follower of the Chasidic master Reb Mottel of Chernobyl had a peculiar habit which came to light when he visited Reb Mottel to request a blessing.

Reb Mottel asked the visitor to recount his typical daily schedule. The young Chasid explained that he began each day by buying goods for his business from the Poretz, the local landowner. Following that, he would recite Shachris, the morning prayers, after which he began to sell his wares.

"Why do you buy your merchandise before you pray in the morning?' asked Reb Mottel.

"Why Rebbe, if I waited until after the prayers, the only goods remaining would be of inferior quality, if not sold out entirely!" The Chasid explained.

Upon hearing that, Reb Mottel said to his young follower, "Let me tell you a story…"

&CR

There was once a Melamed, a teacher of Jewish studies, whose livelihood entailed traveling far from his hometown to teach Jewish children in distant cities. He was often away from his home for a year or more at a time. Meanwhile his wife and children would live the year without him, borrowing and living on credit.

This teacher would be paid for his services with coins. The wealthy would give him gold coins, the middle class paid with silver coins, while people of more modest means paid with copper or nickel coins.

This Melamed had made a belt for himself on which he would hang the various bags. Each bag would carry a different type of coin. He had a bag for his gold coins, a bag for his silver coins, a bag for his nickel coins and a bag for his copper coins.

One time, after his year of teaching was up, he traveled back home. As the first Shabbos on his voyage was quickly approaching, he didn't know where to hide his bags of money.

He decided to bury his earnings in the ground and retrieve them after Shabbos. As he was about to finish his digging, he heard some people in the distance. Paranoia set in, and he became alarmed by the possibility that if he could hear them, they probably saw him and now his money wasn't safe.

He was desperately pressed for time since Shabbos was drawing close. He grabbed the belt with the bags of coins and ran to the local Jewish inn, where he just gave the innkeeper the bundle in a furious hurry for safekeeping. Shabbos began and the Melamed was livid with himself. He had just given the innkeeper his entire year's earnings without a note or receipt mentioning the amount of money being held. It would be so easy for the innkeeper to deny safeguarding the coins, and his whole year's pay would be lost.

Thoughts of his wife and children flooded his mind. What would they do? How will they face the creditors? His imagination took off, leaving him worried, depressed and on edge for the entire Shabbos.

The innkeeper sensed his guest's troubled condition and, as soon as Shabbos departed, he recited Ma'ariv, the evening prayer, very quickly and placed the belt with the bags of coins in front of the teacher who was still reciting the silent Amidah prayer.

To the amazement of the innkeeper, in the middle of his supplications, the teacher opened the bag of gold coins and started counting them one by one. He saw all were there, not one was missing. Nevertheless, he took out the bag with the silver coins and started counting them next. All the silver coins were also there, yet his concern and worry did not dissipate. He then started counting the nickel coins, and then the copper coins. Only after he had counted all the coins did he return his full concentration to his prayer. Stunned, the innkeeper was observing the teacher the whole while, and was perplexed by his behavior.

When the teacher finished his prayers, the innkeeper confronted him. "After you saw I hadn't taken any of your gold coins, why did you not trust that I hadn't taken any of your silver coins that are much less valuable? And after you counted the silver coins too, and saw I took nothing, why didn't you trust me then? You continued to count the ridiculously less valuable nickel and copper coins.

荱荲

Reb Mottel of Chernobyl turned to the young Chasid before him and said, "I want to ask you the same question the innkeeper asked the teacher with the belt of money bags. Every single morning, Hashem has given you back your Neshamah, your soul, and life to your body – the equivalent of gold and silver coins. What makes you think he won't give you your Parnasa, your livelihood – your nickel and copper coins? You should increase your trust, and believe that Hashem will give you your physical sustenance too. There is no need to rush off to buy goods before the morning prayers. Your prayers come first!"

荱荲

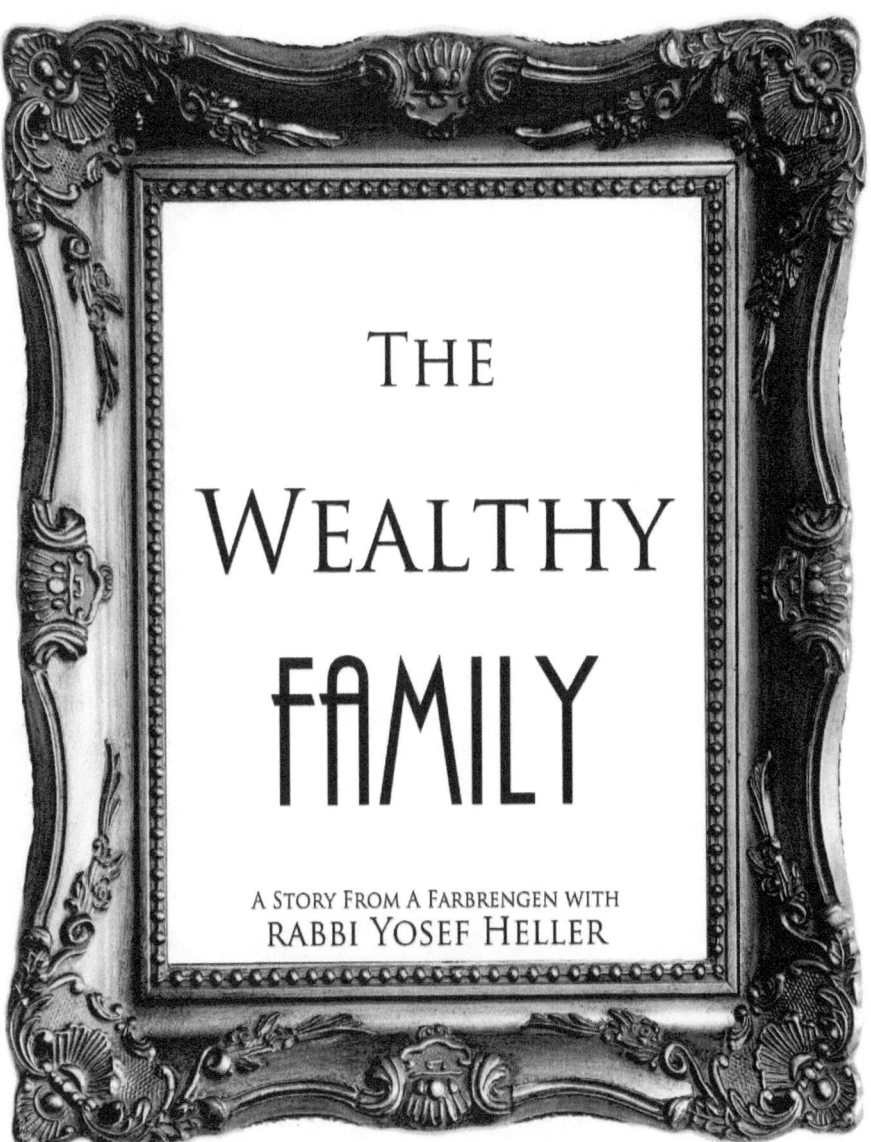

THE

WEALTHY

FAMILY

A STORY FROM A FARBRENGEN WITH
RABBI YOSEF HELLER

One of the more controversial stories served on our Shabbos table has been one I heard at a grand Yud Tes Kislev Farbrengen at Kollel Menachem, **Rabbi Yosef Avraham HaLevi Heller,** *the Rosh Kollel.*

On that special occasion he stressed the importance of creating a personal goal for oneself of serving Hashem simply. This, instead of succumbing to the endless drive of climbing up the heights of recognition and status.

An individual's 'simple' divine service is to be achieved through learning Torah with sincerity, and Davening, praying, with Kavanah, inner meaning and pure intention.

A bold illustration for his advice was encapsulated with the following story he shared.

here was a certain Jew who owned a store whose life was made up of a particular routine. He woke up, learned Torah, Davened Shachris, prayed his morning prayers, and then he went to work. When he came back home at night he spent time with his wife and children, and in addition, he also kept a Kvius, a set time, of learning Torah.

This pattern would repeat itself every day.

Learning Torah was important to this storeowner and he kept his Shiurim, Torah learning sessions, religiously, without fail.

One day, a new store opened up close to this man's store, selling similar stock.

The new store owner threw himself into the business spending much of his time on it and he worked tirelessly to make it a success. The new store not only succeeded, but its growth exploded.

All the while, the man with the original store kept his regular Seder, order of his day, which included learning morning and night and spending quality time with his family.

He adamantly chose not to increase the amount of time working in the slightest, so as not to rob time from his family and learning.

His business suffered as a result of the new store's boom, so instead of having meat or chicken for supper every night he could only afford to buy them for Shabbos. Yet, he didn't alter his treasured usage of time.

The 'new' store owner eventually expanded his growing enterprise by adding multiple store locations and his time was consumed by the business even more.

Even though he was also Frum, a religious Jew, the owner of these stores didn't set times for learning Torah, and he didn't spend so much time with his children either, since the business captivated his full attention.

The focus of these two families was vastly different. The man with the one store made it his goal to spend time with his children and the personal example he set of keeping his Shiurim permeated his home with the message of what is truly important, a Torah centered family life.

The man with the many stores had an altogether different concentration, his business, whose success he was obsessed with. This sent a strong message to his family of what was truly important to him, his financial achievement. Although seemingly 'money could buy everything', the man's tens or hundreds of millions of dollars didn't buy any Nachas from his children, who were negatively affected as a result of their father's misplaced prioritizing. They developed various problems, G-d forbid, such as disregard for Torah and Mitzvos leading to varying levels of disconnection from daily observance of Judaism. Their material excesses led to addictions including debilitating drug problems.

After several years, the rich man got a heart attack from the many stresses of his successful business empire, which literally killed him.

His wife took over, but sadly after several years, the job took its toll and she also died of a stress related illness.

The great fortune that this couple amassed now was to be inherited by their children, however, because of their personal issues and vicious infighting amongst the siblings, the courts froze the assets and the kids didn't get even one penny of the great fortune which their parents sacrificed their lives for. Besides losing the wealth which the parents cared so much for, each one of their children was plagued with personal problems that were directly 'inherited' from the parent's direction (or lack of) in life.

Meanwhile, the 'poorer' family whose father had only one store and dedicated his time to his children, and learning Torah, merited to derive much Nachas from his children who really flourished under their parents attention, guidance and personal example.

The father's set times for learning everyday became like street lamps on the road of his children's life, illuminating their way, showing them what really counts. They married and established Frum Chasidishe homes founded on the beautiful observance of Torah and Mitzvos.

How this father spent his spare time was a truly shrewd investment. It enriched his family tremendously making them genuinely wealthy.

80C3

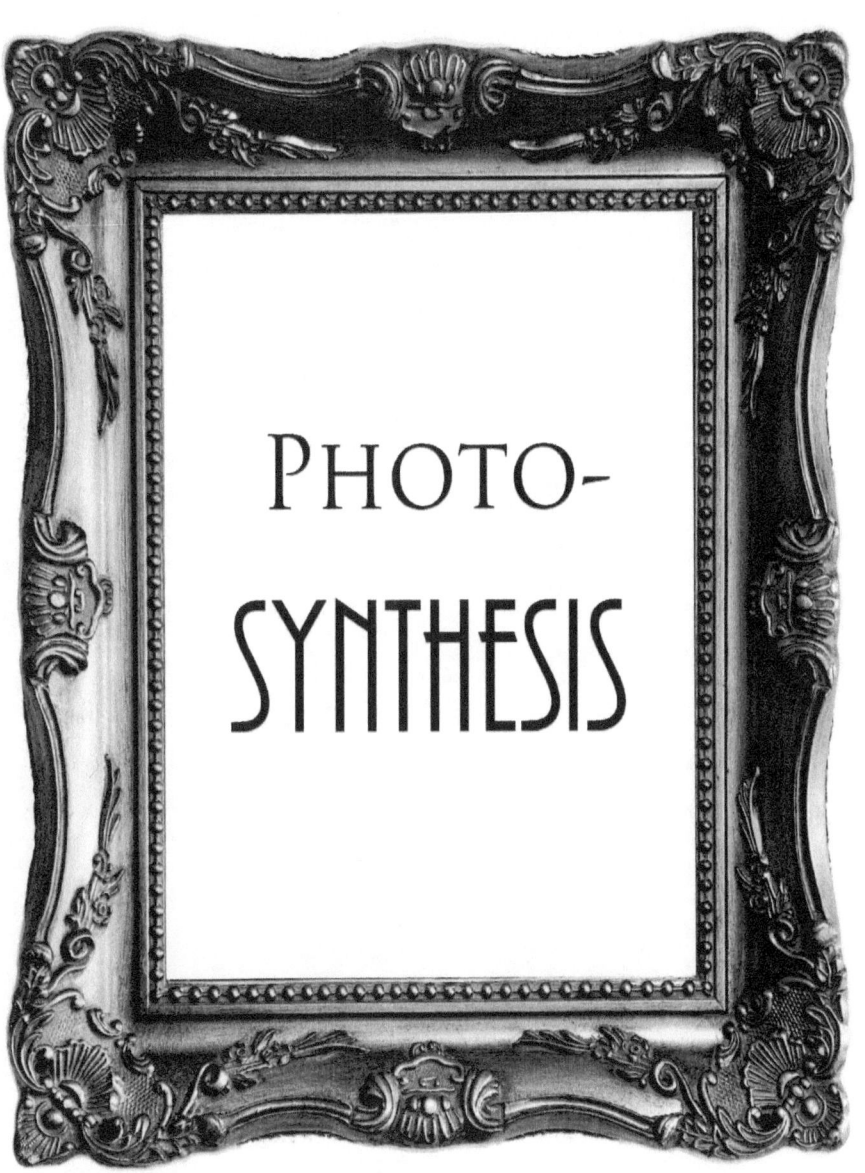

PHOTO-
SYNTHESIS

I t was a regular day in the life of some of New York City's most photographed people. Not in the Seventh Avenue fashion district mind you, but rather in our photo superstore in midtown Manhattan. We Kiosk guides in the store are always surrounded by shutter releases and flash fire set off by photographers admiring the latest and greatest in camera innovations.

But one day, we noticed inquisitive eyes inspecting the kiosk from every angle. Unlike the people who were checking out the Canon photography fantasia, this inspection included us, and the shooters themselves...

"If you need any help, please let me know, "I reached out with a smile of professional courtesy. The Canon executive making this inspection laughed and introduced himself. He had a companion, and I asked if he was from Canon as well.

"No, I'm not from Canon," he said. "I'm from a competing retailer from England. We love your store. What you've done here is just brilliant!" he exclaimed.

"I didn't draw the blueprints for the store, and these are not my ideas. You're complimenting the wrong person," I replied humorously.

He confessed he took many ideas from our store which worked wonderfully for him.

"We come here often," he admitted.

With a slight sense of unease, I ended with another courteous smile. "Ideas are meant to be shared," was what I said, but my thoughts were on our ideas being 'carried' off in someone else's head...

The Canon big wig and his business acquaintance dashed off to investigate the current retail ideas on display. The gentlemen were clearly shopping, although not for products. I replayed the conversation in my head, trying to come to terms with the competitor who borrows ideas from this unique store. As my mind wandered, I realized you don't have to be a multibillion dollar powerhouse to implement this photo business's ideas and see results.

We undergo a semi-uncomfortable process of performance review. The salesmen in our megastore are measured monthly on our courtesy, as our employers emphasize positive interaction with all customers. I came to love the parallel idea of evaluating oneself for courtesy to every person encountered, not just towards customers. How much more pleasant life would be if people borrowed this idea for their personal life? All people should be treated pleasantly. Driven to be courteous to all around me could start a positivity revolution!

If I were to make a 'Personal Life Performance Evaluation Report', perhaps I would include this, 'how courteous was I today with every person I encountered?'

Another big emphasis in our establishment is on having a great conversation with our customers. Our company is seriously focused on making customers and only then sales. If I take this business goal and apply it to everyday life I can surely introduce good energy wherever

I go. My 'Personal Life Performance Report' can include the question: 'have I exerted myself to have great conversations with my family, coworkers, acquaintances and the strangers life throws my way?'

Over time, I came to terms with my unease, both with borrowing these ideas and personal reviews. I admit to copying my employers' progressive ideas to help in my very own family life... The evaluations and daily, weekly and monthly reports we are given here are not just effective for adults, they aid me and my wife with our children. Inspired by these progress reports, we have behavior charts and reward them after they've gained several star stickers for various things. They love this system as it gives them a sense of accomplishment. Incentives for good behavior can work for all ages, whether it's prizes for children or a paycheck for adults.

Luckily, I work in the world's biggest and most successful photo, video, and pro audio retailer. I can copy, borrow or outright take some of these proven business tools and use them in my personal life to become a super success in my very own business, the business of life.

One smile and success story at a time, we transform the rest of the world for good. Viva you! Viva me! Viva personal success!

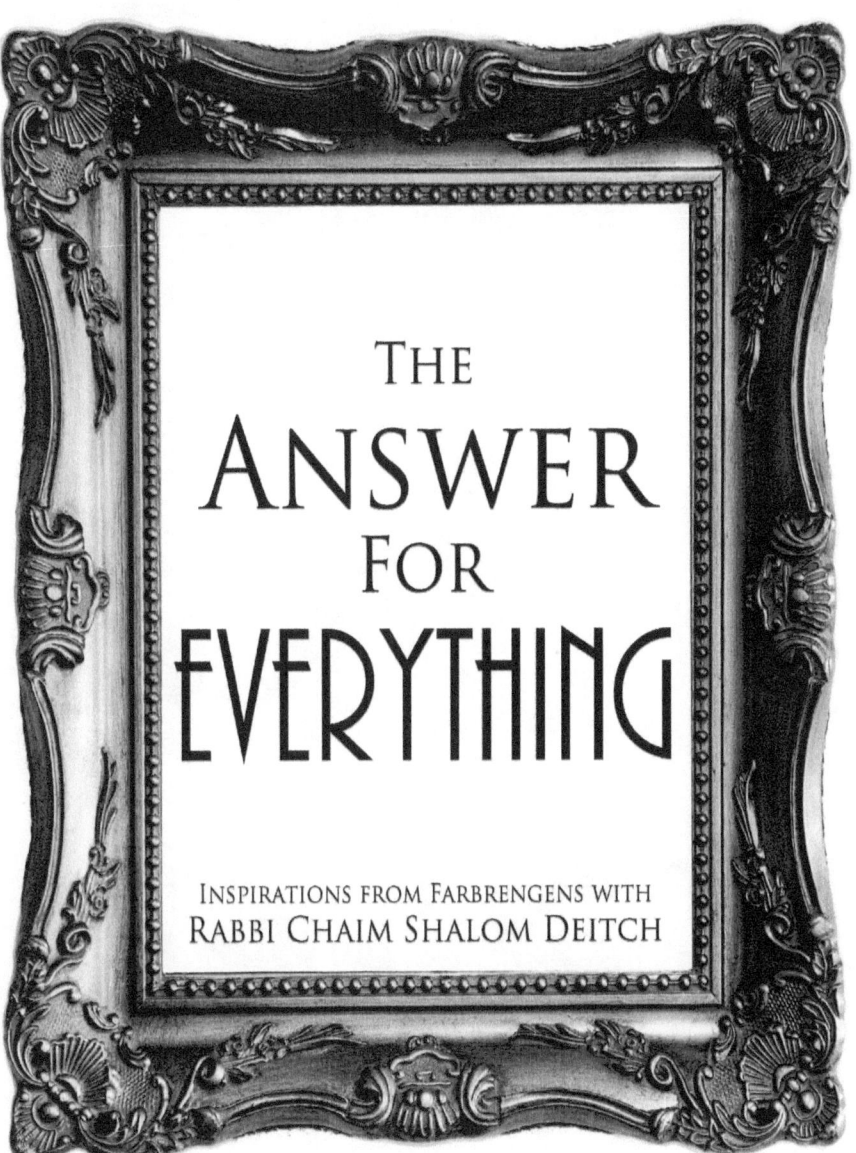

The
ANSWER
For
EVERYTHING

INSPIRATIONS FROM FARBRENGENS WITH
RABBI CHAIM SHALOM DEITCH

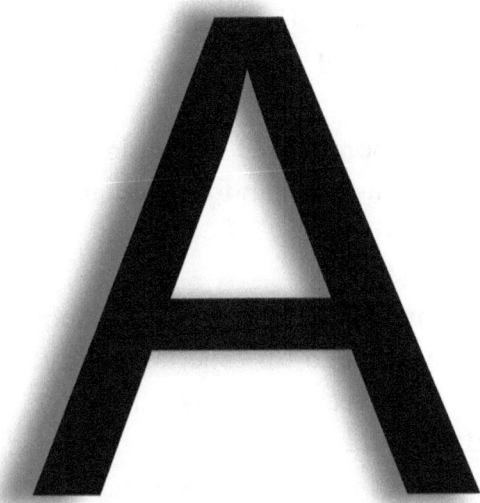

psychologist acquaintance of mine told me a couple of enlightening 'stories' I'd like to share with you.

The first one was presented at a psychologists' conference a number of years ago...

A school teacher woke up extra early one morning to ensure to get to his school on time. Even though he arrived in the station much earlier than the scheduled bus's time of arrival, the bus didn't come.

He was confident that he will get on the next bus; however, the next scheduled bus never came either. Not only did these two buses never arrive, but also the bus after that unfortunately never showed up...

Now he was desperate not only to get to his school early, but just to get there on time.

He kept looking at his watch frantically while the clock kept ticking.

Looking down the street he saw no signs of the bus coming, so he decided to hail a cab instead of waiting fruitlessly.

Soon thereafter, he got a taxi, but he arrived to his school very late nevertheless.

He ran down the corridors of the school darting to his classroom and finally he arrived there breathless and sweaty.

As he entered the classroom one of his students, a little five year old boy, approached him and pointed at his watch.

The teacher was enraged!

He had made so many efforts to get to the school on time. He went to sleep and woke up especially early. He planned on taking an extra early bus, which never came. Not only that but also the following two buses never showed up. He was forced to get a taxi which was terribly expensive for him and nevertheless he was late, despite all of his planning.

Now, after all this, his student was rubbing it in, pointing at his watch indicating how late he was.

He got so angry he felt like letting out all of his emotions on this rude insensitive little boy.

However, this teacher adhered to a personal rule of his.

Whenever he got angry, he wouldn't talk about it for at least five minutes.

Instead of screaming or saying some negative comment, he resolved with himself that whenever he got angry he would hold it in and wait for five minutes until his anger has quieted down, then and only then will he discuss the matter at hand.

He told the boy he couldn't speak to him now but that he should come and speak with him at the end of the class. When the boy came to him at the end of the session the teacher asked him what did he want to tell him earlier.

The boy simply shocked the teacher with his words, "Teacher, I wanted to show you the new watch my parents got for me last night. You are my favorite teacher, so I wanted you to be the first one to see my watch!"

The teacher was stunned.

He had completely and utterly misjudged the situation.

ೞಞ

After the story was presented at the psychologists' conference, the professionals present studied it from various angles.

They concluded that had the teacher punished the boy, or admonished him because of the teacher's own misjudgment, undoubtedly the teacher would have scarred the boy for life introducing serious emotional damage.

The lesson from it was that the teacher's five minute rule saved the boy's emotional life.

BAD STUDENT, GOOD STUDENT

The second 'story' is about an interesting experiment that was conducted exploring the topic of nature vs. nurture. They were testing whether the environment of an individual affects him more than the person's nature or vice versa.

Two classrooms were chosen for this. One class included star students with the highest marks while the other was made up of the weakest students.

The teachers for both classes were given specific instructions:

The teacher of the 'bright' students was not to ever compliment the students, nor encourage or say anything positive at all. She was to give only negative feedback and try to always find fault and criticize amply.

The teacher of the 'below average' students got the exact opposite instructions. This teacher was always supposed to compliment the students, encourage and always say something positive. She had to consistently give positive feedback and try to always find the good in the students.

The students did not realize that they were being experimented on; this was to be a complete secret.

After the year passed they judged the 'surprising' results...

The 'slower' class flourished under the encouraging teacher's treatment. It drastically outperformed the 'clever' kids class who slumped behind and shrunk under the discouraging negative teacher.

The positive 'nurturing' of the students proved more vital than the 'nature' of the student...

‍ఏుపో

UNBOUND

Just yesterday, I met the most remarkable individual. He is a teacher in Oholei Torah who literally transformed an entire class of 'bad' boys.

Apparently, everyone had given up hope on these kids, not only the school system but also their very own parents. Yet when this teacher was given the 'coveted' job of educating these kids who were labeled as lost cases, he astounded everyone by actually succeeding.

How did he do it? How did this teacher reach these kids when everyone else failed miserably?

I asked him what his secret was.

He answered, "I simply saw past the stifling labels their previous teachers and very own parents put on them. Instead of treating them as bad kids, or even as Nebachs, sorry cases, I tried to see the good, look inside them, past all the baggage. I ignored the constricting categorizations and boxes they were put into while concentrating purely on their essence. I tried to see them for who they really are, amazing, brilliant and sharp children with unlimited potential. Addressing them in a positive light, with Hashem's help, was what brought out their true selves and created a space for them to grow and learn!"

I AM A HERO!

I heard of a true story regarding a high minister in the Israeli government who used to make a habit of visiting the Rebbe on his diplomatic trips to New York.

Whenever he would come in for a Yechidus, a private audience, with the Rebbe, he always left amazed with himself at how he so casually revealed the most secret of operations.

The Rebbe just had a knack of getting him to talk as if he was merely a child.

One time he strongly decided that he will not divulge confidential information anymore. After all, he was not a toddler! He was a high official in the Israeli government!

Before he came in to see the Rebbe he repeated to himself again and again this affirmation, "I am a high official in the government. I can hold myself from telling state secrets. I am not a child. I am a high official in the government...."

There is a powerful verse that says, "Hakatan Yumar Gibor Ani!"(Yoel 4,10), "The weak should say I am great!'

Sometimes we don't have that special someone to encourage us. We can find ourselves without a supportive cultivating teacher to help us grow, or even our parents or siblings cannot offer much needed moral support.

It's quite possible that a warm word from friends, or for that matter friends themselves, are lacking and are just not available.

Then the responsibility lies on our very own shoulders to encourage and strengthen ourselves repeatedly, just like that minister.

No matter how small we might seem, 'Katan', the verse teaches us that we should declare to ourselves confidently, "Gibor Ani!" I am a hero! I can do this!

THE CURE

A certain man felt an overall lack of strength, and even weakness, so he went to the doctor.

After the checkup, the doctor suggested the man start eating a certain type of grapes as a cure. The man immediately went to the grocery store and bought a bunch of those prescribed grapes. Immediately upon his return home he took out one grape and ate it.

After he ate the grape he flexed his muscles and analyzed how he felt now. Unfortunately he did not feel any better.

Undeterred, he proceeded to take another grape and again checked himself for any improvement, but there was none. Before he gave up on the doctor's recommended cure he decided to try taking one more grape. He took the grape and chewed it slowly hoping this would do it, this grape will cure him. To his great disappointment also the third grape did not help.

The man went to the doctor the next day and complained that his prescription, the grapes, did not cure him. The doctor asked him how he came to this conclusion. The man described exactly what he did, to the amusement of the doctor.

After the man finished, the doctor explained to him that if he wants to be cured, he needs to eat many grapes over an extended period of time. One grape or for that matter three grapes, are not going to do it!

The Tzemach Tzedek said that there are three things that if one has enough of, it's guaranteed that they will produce a change.

The first thing is wealth. If a person amasses enough financial success, at some point, they will change.

The second thing is liquor. If someone drinks, if they drink more and more, at some point, surely they will get drunk.

The third thing is Chasidus. If an individual learns Chasidus, continually, it's impossible to remain unchanged, they will be transformed.

Likewise, when a couple builds a home, for it to be a Chasidish home there are several things on the to do list:

1) Learning Torah with oneself.

2) Learning Torah with one's spouse (this is very important since the married couple must talk to each other, by Torah learning with one another they introduce Kedusha, holiness, into their dialogue, into their relationship).

3) Participating in Farbrengens regularly (this is vital and shouldn't be underestimated, since this is a tremendous tool for Chasidim to strengthen each other both personally and spiritually).

Each holy endeavor or action is like a grape which contributes to the overall picture. One or two are not enough, but if you do them plentifully and frequently, with Hashem's help, you'll have a house that radiates Chasidic light.

CHASIDISH IS NOT ENOUGH !

When asked about what he is looking for in a Shiduch, the Bochur answered that the most important attribute for him was that the girl should be Chasidish.

"Chasidish is not enough!" Declared Rabbi Deitch.

The Bochur defended his answer saying that he thought that being Chasidish entails all good aspects in a life mate.

Rabbi Deitch immediately negated the Bochur's reasoning.

His unexpected answer placed the ambiguous definition of 'Chasidish' under interesting scrutiny.

He explained that a 'spiritual individual' could Daven at length, learn a lot, perform Mitzvos Be'Hiddur, beautifully, and overall seem to be 'connected' to Hashem. However, all the while, he could be exhibiting negative traits to fellow individuals such as lack of compassion, respect or the warmth of friendliness. (This doesn't mean that a person is either this or that, but unfortunately, one doesn't guarantee the other.)

Essentially, a person could be very nice to Hashem, while being not very nice to people.

It is most important while looking for a Shiduch to research how good are they to, and with people, not just to Hashem.

Is she nice to people in general? How does she get along with her peers? Is she a kind person who helps the people around her?

The prospect's Middos, personal attributes, are probably the most important aspects to be researching while looking for a Shiduch.

In marriage you are dealing with a human being whose traits you will be living with on an everyday basis.

To ensure Shalom Bais, a peaceful union, you need to inquire whether she has the potential (based on past history) to be nice, good natured and giving.

'Chasidishkeit' is a good start, however good Middos, and their cultivation throughout one's life, are crucial for building a Binyan Adei Ad, a strong long-lasting edifice.

(Although addressed to a Bochur, seemingly, all this also applies to woman as well...)

INTIMATE KNOWLEDGE

There is a Halacha that states individuals should begin immersing themselves into the learning of the laws and customs for the upcoming holiday thirty days before it occurs (Shulchan Aruch Admor Hazaken 429, 1-3). Those days are a necessary period of time of preparation for the upcoming holiday. The proper observance of the holiday can only be fulfilled with the essential knowledge and awareness of its substantial amount of details and nuances.

How can you do something if you don't even know it exists? How can you perform something in an acceptable manner if you aren't sufficiently proficient or intimately familiar with its many components?

If we designate a full month for the adequate review of the laws of a holiday, which comes around but once a year, surely this could be applied to the holy Shabbos, which reoccurs every week. With its immense amount of intricate laws and customs, an individual should also be preparing for the Shabbos 'thirty days prior to it...'

However, since Shabbos comes weekly, it is a vital need for us to constantly learn and review its Halachos to satisfactorily observe this holy day in a complete, beautiful and a befitting fashion!

The great importance of the mastery of the Halachos of Shabbos is highlighted by the Alter Rebbe on the very last page of the Tanya. There he writes, "...Whoever observes the Shabbos according to its laws is pardoned for all his sins. 'According to its laws', specifically (since the Shabbos cannot be observed properly without acquiring the knowledge of its laws). It is therefore a responsibility, placed upon every individual, to master the great law(s) of Shabbos..."

ဆၢ

LIGHTS WITHOUT VESSELS

It was a chilly wintry day during which I really didn't want to travel to the funeral. I forced myself nevertheless since I knew this Chasid. He passed away several years ago; however his body was being relocated to a different gravesite.

I have been to another burial similar to this and the stench of the decomposing body was unbearable. I was surprised that this funeral was different. This man didn't stink! His body was intact. Usually, this kind of thing is found only by Tzadikim, yet he externally seemed like an ordinary man.

He was not a famous Tzadik. He was just a 'simple man' yet his actions were extraordinary. He was committed to Mivtzoim (Mitzvah campaigns) of the Rebbe and was always occupied helping others. Whether it was learning with people one on one, affixing Mezuzahs, or assisting in Kashering a home, he was always busy with Mitzvos.

He was not an official Shliach or Rav. He was not officially part of any organization. He was without any formal 'vessels', however his life was all about sharing light. The lack of vessels didn't stop him, if anything; it made his light limitless.

୫୦୧୪

THE ANSWER FOR EVERYTHING
PERSONAL REFLECTIONS FROM A FARBRENGEN

At the beginning of a major Farbrengen in Kfar Chabad where Rabbi Deitch was the main speaker he stood up and started by declaring that Likutei Torah (by the Alter Rebbe) on the Parsha contains the answer for everything!

He enumerated several specific problems as his examples.

The most memorable one was without a shadow of a doubt Machshavos Zaros, impure thoughts. The reason that this particular topic comes to the forefront of my mind is because a senior Chasid present, who was also a featured speaker, interrupted Rabbi Deitch's speech and dramatically opposed him. He stated that Rabbi Deitch shouldn't attempt to change people on a personal front, claiming the Rabbi will definitely not affect any change in his Machshavos Zaros, but rather he should concentrate the speech on more lofty ideals, such as Shlichus!

This outburst and opposition clearly validated for me just how important Rabbi Deitch's words truly were because they clearly were touching sensitive buttons. He specifically chose to personalize Chasidus as a catalyst for change, both personal and global. For him it is not cosmetic. He affirmed how spiritual self-neglect doesn't help accomplish or satisfy an individual's cosmic mission in life even while masquerading behind noble acts... A Chasid has to invest in himself seriously and actively work on personal change internally, not just talk about lofty ideals; he has to authentically live it.

This charmed and charming masterful Torah scholar who seems to almost always wear a friendly smile does nothing but inspire and truly teaches on many levels how the learning of Torah in general and Chasidus in particular could be 'the answer for everything'. However, he stresses and exemplifies that all of the learning is not for check marking it as 'I learned it, I know it already' or only to adorn one's mind with lofty concepts that provide a spiritual trip, but rather it has to be sincerely and positively applied to everyday life on a personal level.

That is the answer for everything…

ജാര

In merit of Devorah Bas Simon.

BLOODY

WINTER

ike clockwork, every year around winter time, the skin over my knuckles cracks and bleeds.

This phenomenon started over a decade ago, on the occasion of the first wedding I was commissioned to photograph.

Back then I was just excited to land the job, I had no idea I was going to get a long-lasting 'souvenir'.

As the bride glossed over my portfolio, she declared she 'loved' my creativity and insisted that she could have any photographer she wanted. She said money was no object and I, not knowing any better, was eager to believe her.

It was so flattering to be chosen out of all the professionals, the real photographers, considering I was just 'starting', surely my talent spoke for itself.

Not knowing the prices for wedding photography, we settled on only $500 (not including the expenses of film or its development; yes, this was pre digital…) which should've tipped me off right away that something just wasn't right, as most other photographers charge loads more.

My best friend at the time was to serve as the second photographe and we were happy to split the small 'fortune' fifty-fifty considering we were both just rabbinic students at the time, making do with bare minimum. Both of us felt we scored big with this lucrative deal and were surfing on a high wave.

With luck on our side, the night of the wedding was hailed as the coldest night of the decade, or was it the century?

It was cold, really really cold.

The ceremony was, of course, held outside, with the black skies above us and the numbing chilly air serving as a blanket, covering the shivering cool crowd.

There we were, both running around like two Meshoganes, crazy people, documenting the event as it was unfolding in the most photojournalistic way known to us. We were using a mixture of color and black and white film to photograph a crowd that included women who wore colored clothes and men who were wearing black and white.

I noticed that the gloves that I was wearing seemed to get in the way, so I removed them and was relieved to find that all the camera's controls were now accessible and comfortably under my control.

As the minutes advanced, and as I advanced the film, my fingers were getting colder and colder.

At one point in the middle of the ceremony, as I was changing film, I was shocked to see that my hands were covered with blood, my own blood.

The extremely low temperature had stung my virgin hand skin producing dark stains of blood on my hands which also dripped onto my camera.

Soon after I learned my hands were bleeding, I started noticing that I couldn't feel my fingers anymore, my hands were frozen!

In the midst of the climax of the wedding ceremony I couldn't run out to care for myself, or just run away period, I was stuck in a situation that reeked of disaster, meanwhile all I could think of was the bride and groom and how important this event was for them.

Instead of giving the bare minimum I strongly felt I had to give the most I could possibly give in all ways possible.

Rubbing my hands or putting the gloves back on didn't help any, but miraculously enough, I managed to get by with pressing the shutter button, but there was one problem...

An extreme paranoia had set in me, I believed that I either had already broken my fingers, or that I might break my fingers while operating the camera.

Was I pressing the shutter button too strongly? Was my wrestling with the film door to change rolls of film jeopardizing my bones?

My failed attempts at opening the film door added another layer of desperation to my introduction to wedding photography, which by now proved to be a bona fide nightmare.

My friend, the second photographer, was snapping away somewhere beyond my reach or calls for help, so I resorted to breaking whatever professional decorum I was holding onto, and asked one of the guests to help me out.

I explained that my fingers were frozen solid and that I needed urgent assistance to open the film door, remove the used film and insert a new roll into the camera.

This heaven sent photo assistant enabled me to keep snapping, changing roll after roll, all the while, I did not know if I was photographing with broken fingers...

"I'll know if they are ok in the hall" I said to myself as I kept looking for interesting moments to immortalize.

Finally at the hall, my fingers were resurrected with some warm water which also washed away all evidence of any artistic self-sacrifice.

I started to feel them and I was overjoyed to discover that I hadn't broken anything. I sighed a sigh of relief, thank G-d, all was well!

After the experience of a photographic work hazard, the evening progressed beautifully, while the only witness to my personal plight outdoors at the ceremony was the guest, the angel who helped me, who danced the night away while I clicked the shutter away.

A few days after the wedding, I excitedly delivered the rolls of film. Soon thereafter, I was asked to attend an emergency meeting with the newlyweds.

My naïve expectations were sky high, perhaps a generous tip for the outstanding job we performed against all odds, however instead I got something, umm, quite different.

The young couple was furious with me. I was stunned and speechless.

Apparently, the angry couple didn't anticipate thirty rolls of film, even though they did mention quietly, in passing, that they did love the rolls they did develop.

Instead of being saluted with lavish praise for going all out, which I was expecting, I had to deal with a young couple who wanted to eat me alive, because they just didn't want to pay to develop all the film!

I worked too hard and gave them too many pictures. Instead of valuing the extra strips of film, they were having a blast letting off steam by whipping me with the negatives.

I somehow neutralized the crazy scene in their tiny kitchen by saying I was never asked to limit my output, and in addition I was under the impression that they cared about quality and creativity, so I gave my very best. Most people would pay a lot more for all this. If anything, some whould complain of not having enough pictures or that their photographer hadn't worked hard...

I got the rest of the money, aside for the deposit before the wedding, and I heard through the grapevine, to top it all off, that this couple was giving me free publicity, they were telling people not to use me.

A few years after this wedding I met the groom who smiled at me and proudly declared he still didn't develop all the rolls of film from his wedding.

I have to say I was completely taken aback by the lack of appreciation for all my efforts. If he already had the rolls of his own wedding, and he admitted that they were stunning (I have to take his word for it since I never got to see them), what point was he proving by not developing all of them and letting these memories collect dust? I just didn't get it.

That first wedding was an undeniably explosive crash course in the bittersweet inner dynamics, and potential traumatic mishaps of event photography, business and human relations.

Looking back, I can only shrug my shoulders. But, honestly speaking, I am most amazed with myself that I ever touched a camera again.

If only I had known about contracts which clarify expectations.

If only I had known about reasonable pricing and not been taken advantage of.

If only I had been more prepared and bought some photographers gloves.

If only I had developed the film myself so I could see my pictures.

If only I had developed a few of the images to showcase them in my portfolio.

If only I had done all these things, but I didn't, alas, it was the first time I declared 'I hate photography'...

Nevertheless, with all of its and my shortcomings, I did it! My first big job! I did the best I could (I have improved since then). And I was proud of myself, even though I had to deal with a situation that was beyond difficult in almost every way.

Every winter since then, I get a bloody reminder of that wedding ceremony, since it seems that the skin on my hands doesn't want me to forget.

Perhaps it's just a random souvenir of one of my first major jobs, which I barely, yet miraculously survived. However, my Rabbinic training has made me look at everything with transcendental eyes, making me believe that surely there's a special meaning to everything, also to this.

After some thought I came up with a personal insight. I concluded that it's not just a reminder but a lesson about personal triumph.

Based on this little escapade, I've invented my own definition of personal victory.

When I give my very best, under even occasionally horrible conditions, even if these efforts are underappreciated by others or receive little notice, that is personal triumph and victory!

That is because the goal is, essentially, to do all I can, to do the right thing.

৪৩৫৪

Inspired by the Baal Shem Tov's teaching that from all one sees and hears, from all of one's experiences, a person should apply it as a lesson in Avodas Hashem, serving G-d; my personal lesson takes a deeper more particular twist.

Cosmically speaking, for a Jew, 'to do the right thing' means to do G-d's will, which is comprised of the actual performance of His Mitzvos, the commandments, and the learning of His Torah, every person according to their own level and capabilities.

This task could, at times be met with harsh challenges from our surroundings, and also from within, that threaten to freeze any attempt to connect ourselves with the divine, with opposition as fierce as a painfully cold winter.

It's not coincidental that the Shulchan Aruch, the monumental work that codifies Jewish laws that encompass the basic requirements of every Jew throughout life, mentions in its very first law an interesting foundational teaching.

"An individual shouldn't be ashamed of fulfilling G-d's commandments because of scoffers."

Being laughed at or looked down upon for doing a Mitzvah creates a very harsh environment that could not only 'inspire' someone to just do the bare minimum rather than their very best in effort and intent, it could eradicate everything, G-d forbid.

Hence the first Halacha, law, includes this vital guideline which could enable everything else, being and living Judaism in a proud and expansive manner because of the ultimate importance in the actual performance of all the Mitzvos. Even if, and despite the fact that, instead of receiving praise, an individual receives a chilly rebuke by friends, family or others.

A person might also feel alone in his plight in the freezing cold, attempting to ascend in their spirituality, however there is always the Creator of heaven and earth, that One witness and constant Helper, even in a winter night, that might be the coldest of the decade or century,. He surely appreciates and applauds any such act of kosher connection to Him.

Since the actual performance of Mitzvos and learning our Torah is our spiritual job here on earth, the career that precedes anything else, my personal victory definition could be refined to apply a more specific perspective.

When a Jew is moved to do their utmost, sincerely, in any realm of Torah and Mitzvos, whether they are 'advanced' or just 'starting,' even if these efforts are underappreciated by others or receive little positive notice, no matter how small a Mitzvah it might seem to be or no matter how insignificant a detail of a mitzvah one may pay special attention to, every such deed is a personal triumph!

That is because our highest goal is, essentially, to do all we can do, in our everyday life, to do G-d's will, to be victorious against all odds.

८ාওর

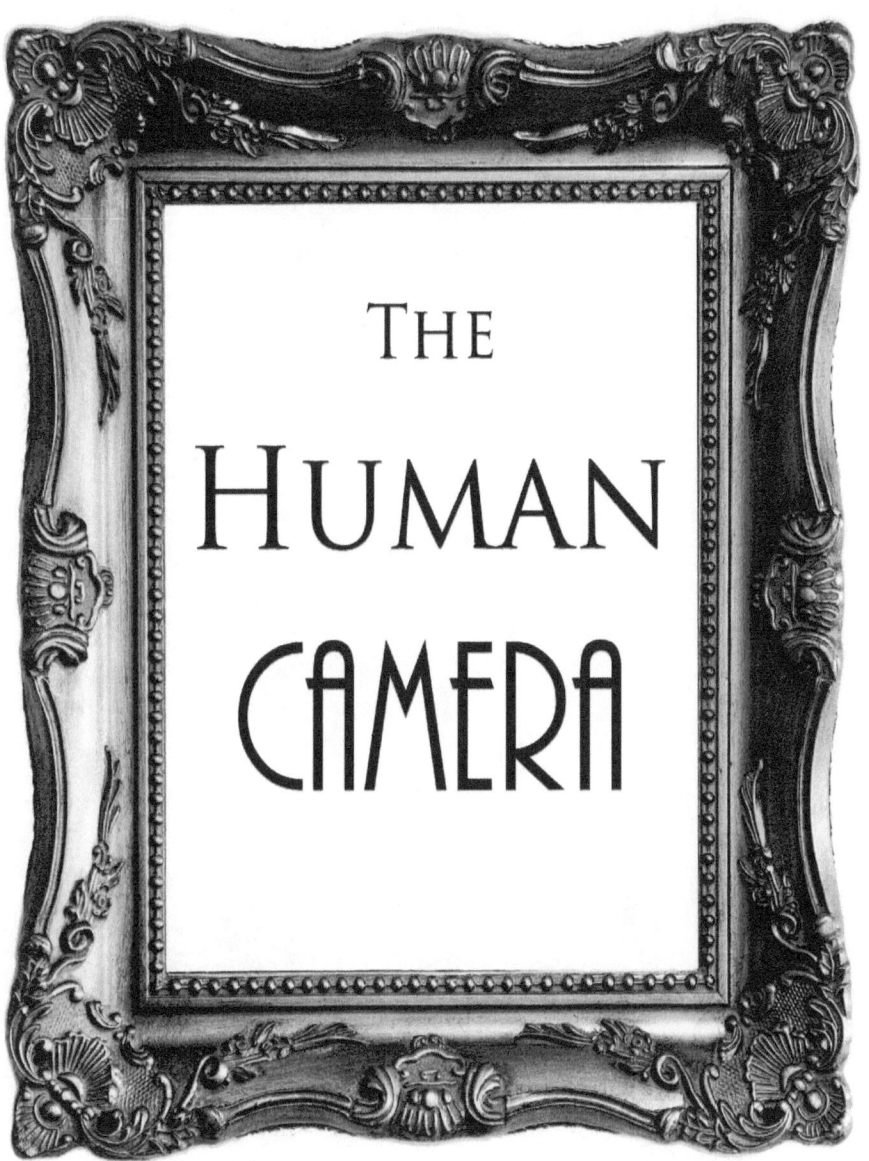

THE

HUMAN

CAMERA

PART 1:
AN INTRODUCTION TO APPLIED PHOTOGRAPHY

veryone is a photographer! We constantly take pictures which define our experiences and share them with the world around us. This occurs regardless of if it translates to actual pictures or image imprints in one's mind.

Cameras, merely being visual vessels taking in the light in view and recording it, are very much like us humans, who absorb from our environments and are, to a large extent, its products. Our personal perspectives are attained through basic functions, just like a camera system.

It's easy for the amateur human or novice camera user to fall in love with the automatic style of life, however, our goal should be to wean ourselves away from the primal 'easy' mode.

Handing an SLR camera (single lens reflex; a sophisticated camera with interchangeable lenses and a reflex mirror enabling the photographer to see through the lens), a tractate on advanced mathematics or philosophical literature to a beginner, besides being intimidating, will rarely create a welcoming urge to learn or improve in any measure without the prerequisite education.

Many users will just opt to employ the easy automatic settings on a small point and shoot (pocket camera), letting the cameras built-in calculations be the boss and essentially do everything.

Similarly, many humans will continue reacting to various situations they encounter by merely a primal instinct, their nature, instead of taking charge and managing their inner settings manually.

It's necessary for us to realize that auto pilot leads to average results most of the time.

To produce amazing pictures that really shine, a person must take charge and manage the camera functions manually. Without taking charge of life's functions, automatic reactions inevitably follow, resulting in poor to average life experiences.

A novice will still ask: "Why upgrade? Photography is an art and life is an art. Better camera equipment and more sophisticated study of life don't make an artist. Let me find my own way through life and photography. Learning from others or learning to use high tech equipment is a time consuming and expensive process... I'd rather keep it simple and just have fun."

Sometimes a question can't be answered with words alone. The person may need to be shown and then the question answers itself. One simple snapshot demonstrated in auto-mode versus manual mode, contrasting the vast quality difference as well as a random result, versus a photograph fully in control of its own beauty, can spark the desire to do better. Just as a tweak of a human's life using education versus ignorant habit can introduce vast improvements that make a major tangible difference.

It's obviously not about which model camera. It's about better pictures. A point and shoot can also be tweaked to get the best output from it without buying an SLR. However, the resulting shortcomings in image quality leave many people wanting more. Yes, 'it's all about the photographer's eye and artistry', but better equipment will produce better pictures because they possess ingredients that enable the user to achieve much more. The sensors are much bigger, the lenses can be swapped to specific optics for a wide variety of effects; the camera is able to capture great resolution with speed that captures life's fleeting moments leaving the smaller point-and-shoots in the dust, most of the time quite literally.

My father is a noted professor, and as a kid I was mortified when he stopped for small talk with a guard of a gated community we were visiting. He was naturally much too important to associate with 'small people', in my then-childish opinion. I questioned him about this interaction and asked him why did he engage this simple man in such an equal, friendly conversation, after all wasn't he so much more important than the gatekeeper?

My father surprised me with his answer stating that each person is important. He said he saw only a man like himself, guarding a lonely gate, in need of a cheerful conversation. He was happy he was able to lift the guard's spirits.

I saw from this, and many other occasions, that my father doesn't live life in auto ego mode; he dials his options to give everyone the dignity they deserve, regardless of their academic excellence, or place of employment.

This brings us to a profound lesson to learn and internalize... It's not the subject, it's the photographer!

A good photographer can make anything look amazing, no matter how ordinary or simple the subject matter. Composition, lighting, angle of view and conceptual ideas are all methods we use to make the ordinary extraordinary. This does require more effort and work than a casual snapshot.

Judging people in life as ordinary, beneath one's notice or to be avoided is not due to any fault of theirs, it's because a person's eye is not trained properly. If an individual attempts to only highlight the good qualities of people, leaving their failings in the shadows, and put effort into appreciating a scene instead of projecting a rash judgment onto it, humbling new vistas of possibility could be discovered.

With the human camera, upgrading the body and internal eye with a better camera and unique optics while utilizing them manually will render much better results than the built-in-at-birth auto settings. 'Manual labor' rewards significantly more than the easy lazy auto mode...

An educated and more refined human will capture and experience humanity in a deeper, more sophisticated and useful light. Exercising the heart and mind through thought and deliberation, with practice will enable a greater and more balanced give and take from life. Our reaction to life's events will leave no detail unappreciated.

The result will be a world of much better imagery.

PART 2:

CHANGE COMES FROM SETTINGS WHITHIN

The first stage of our comparison was between point-and-shoot cameras to SLR cameras, on one hand, and auto modes to manual ones, on the other. These two comparisons correlate and illustrate the undeveloped human to the fully actualized individual on the path of personal refinement.

The second stage involves the controls of the camera, which help fine-tune the idea, letting us take these exercises of inner focus and develop them a few steps further.

The major players on this train of thought analogy are the aperture (the opening in the lens), the shutter speed (the time the light is allowed to enter the sensor) and the ISO (International Organization for Standardization, which is the sensor's light sensitivity).

What are the counterparts of aperture, shutter speed and ISO in a human?

There is no one answer for this question since depending on the situation or the individual they can be different things at different times.

My personal insight on these modes liken the aperture to the mind, the shutter speed to desire and the ISO to the heart, one possible combination out of many…

I hope that you will reflect on it, personalize it and utilize your own symbolism that tailor to you specifically. Naturally, every person's creativity and development is different, as is every photographer's preference of camera settings and lens.

However, it's important to note that these 'three pillars of a photograph' are present and work in unison in every single camera, from the simplest to the most sophisticated.

Overall, the manual setting of a human camera, while looking through the appropriate lens, can enable the deliberate increase of light to enter the camera from a specific one of these controls which can bring about positive results even in low lit situations where the lack of light introduces hardships and frustrations.

This potential of inner control empowers an individual, the human camera, to take a beautiful picture of life in almost any condition.

APERTURE OF THE MIND

The aperture is the size of the opening of the diaphragm inside the lens. By using the wider apertures, the background of the subject can be blurred beautifully; isolating the subject from its environment and making it stand out. The narrower apertures make everything sharp, background and foreground alike.

Minds are wonderful at narrowing our point of focus, or expanding our horizons, as we choose.

Experimenting with apertures allows us to play with the depth of field, the area of the picture that appears in focus.

To see the big picture we choose a smaller aperture which renders greater depth of field in which more (or most) of the image appears to be sharp and in focus.

To see the details of one area over another requires a wider aperture which renders a shallower depth of field in which a narrower area appears in focus while its foreground and background are deemphasized and blurred.

(Although the direction provides the opposite effect - the mind opens wide to see more or attain deep focus and closes to attain shallow focus, the aperture opens wide to get shallow focus and closes to see more or get deep focus - we can attribute that to the reversal of light in picture-taking, as the image strikes the sensor upside down.)

Depending on the current situation, or challenge, we must adjust our aperture. A previously used aperture might not be the answer for right now.

You can open up the aperture, open your mind, or close down the aperture, concentrate!

Opening your mind could include being more accepting, positive and gaining more knowledge. We should not be victims of the choices of our mind's concentration. It's our decision to go big or small, wide or narrow. We are quite capable of choosing our mind's subject of attention.

Close down the mind's aperture to concentrate on a certain subject, blurring out any distractions in the background, or open wide to allow scrutiny of every detail of the entire world-image before you.

Either use of depth-of-field could be used at will depending on the needed effect.

The control of what we choose to focus on determines our experience of the world.

THE DESIRE FOR SHUTTER SPEED

The shutter is the most quickly moving part of the camera. This curtain over the sensor allows us to capture from the most transient of moments to the impression of moving time, compressed into one image. (The sensor is the 'computer chip' on which all the image information is rendered. Previously, there was film.)

A fast shutter speed will freeze action but requires more light; slower speeds allow more light in, but leave action as a motion blur.

We act on our desires, our wishes, but our desires are as adjustable as anything else. Moving fast can get us what we want faster, but moving slowly sheds more light on our desire and gives us time to think. In human terms a person can increase the desire for light, and turn away from dead end desires in a dark moment. Slowing down the shutter allows more light to enter. Slow down to shed more light on a situation, to figure out how to overcome the opposition and obstacles before us, or perhaps to admit that this path should be blocked. Increasing desire to be involved in more light-filled activities can open up core inner elements such as kindness, sympathy and joy.

A fast shutter speed is best used in bright situations with plenty of light were motion can be frozen. Transferring this to real life, in a situation with much light the desire can be directed to accentuate and appreciate every second of life. Take it all in, as fast as you want.

Directing our desires, depending on the moment at hand, can help create the most desired effect throughout life's constantly ever-changing movements.

ISO OF THE HEART

The light sensitivity of the sensor is measured by the ISO setting. A higher number makes the camera's sensor more sensitive to light. In bright situations, lower ISO numbers are set, so the picture doesn't become overexposed, becoming overly white. Higher ISO numbers allow the camera to take pictures in low light conditions so they don't appear underexposed or overly dark. But the higher ISO comes with a certain sacrifice. Lower sensitivity delivers a clearer picture, while with higher ISOs visual noise will appear, creating a grainy picture instead of a clear and smooth one.

The ISO represents the heart in my comparison. A person can increase the level of sensitivity, open up the heart to other people and increase the level of sensitivity to the needed degree. A beautiful image of a person can be achieved even in low light by the right combination of these inner settings, no matter how dark the subject matter.

Opening the heart to really dark places and scenarios introduces some loss of comfort and can go against our grain. Yes, increasing the sensitivity to higher levels introduces noise and grain on the images, discomfort and an exploration of areas where there is lack of clarity, but it's essential to live fully and have unlimited picture-taking opportunities. Without this opening up of the heart, top performance as a human will be impossible, just as a photographer loses photographic opportunities by avoiding photographing in darker, lowlight situations, where higher ISO sensitivity usage is essential.

To truly explore life's entire spectrum of opportunity, let us all adjust the ISO of the heart and help transform dark scenes into magnificent masterpieces.

POINTS OF VIEW

The camera is only able to do as much as the attached lens allows.

There are many different lenses at one's disposal. Wide angle lenses enable taking in sweeping views of landscapes, interiors or families. Telephoto lenses enable reaching faraway subjects or to get real close ups. To get even closer, extremely close, macro lenses do the job. There are faster lenses (due to their bigger apertures that let in more light, they enable the use of faster shutter speeds), zoom lenses moving between angles of view and fixed lenses which feature exclusively one angle, lenses that move horizontally or vertically, and more.

The human camera, as well, has a wide range of perspectives to explore, and it too is limited by the attached lens's perspective...

A wide angle shows the larger picture. Faraway objects require zooming in close. Inspecting a tiny detail of life, calls for a macro lens. Some people's perspectives are brighter, some are darker; some move more, some less. Each perspective creates an attitude, forms an experience, a character, and although they seem immutable, they aren't, we can swap out the lens for another. We can change our perspective, the lens we currently view our life through, for another.

Owning the best camera and lenses available, isn't enough! A person must actually use their camera to attain the great imagery.

Likewise, in one's personal sphere, better education, inspiration and potential is not enough!

An individual must push their knowledge and capabilities into action, into their everyday, to truly achieve a refined life.

Getting good results from seeing and making observations, like any other craft, requires much practice.

In photography, and in photogenic living, individuals are invited to look at the world around them and give it their best shot.

Happy photographing!

ಃಖಣ

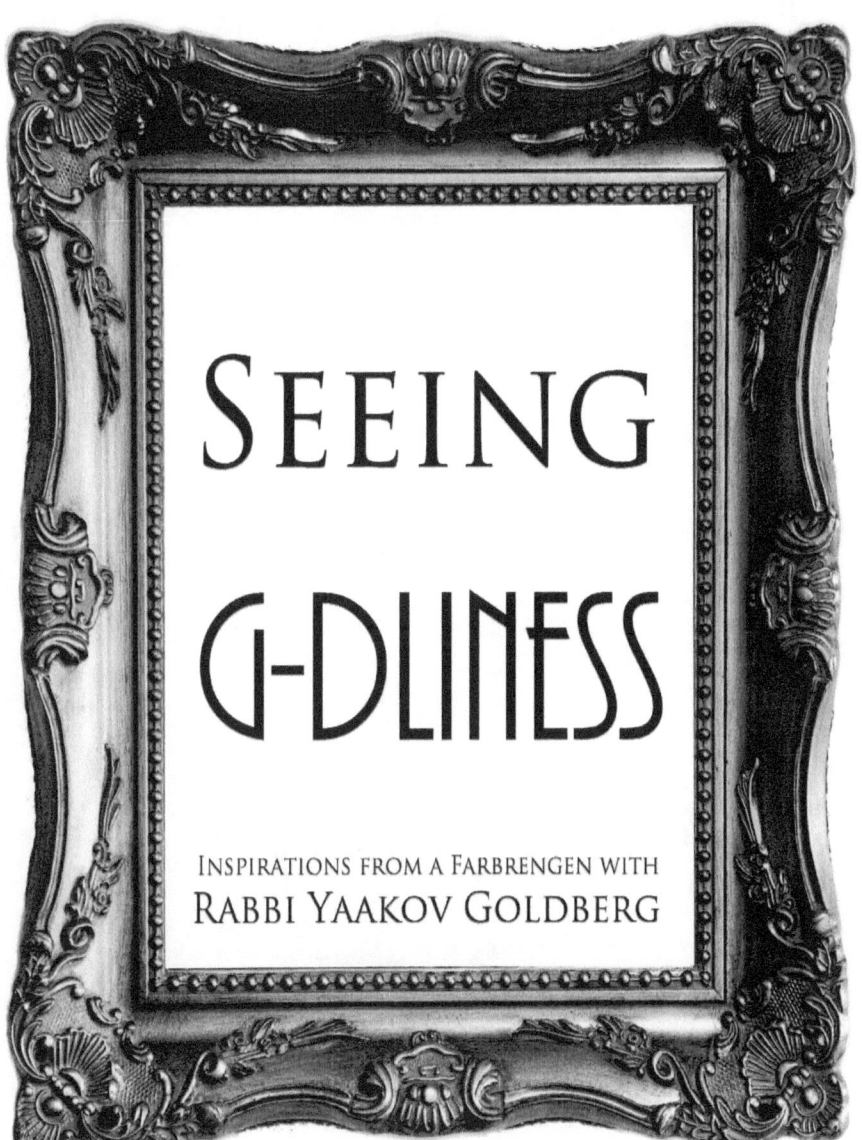

SEEING

G-DLINESS

INSPIRATIONS FROM A FARBRENGEN WITH
RABBI YAAKOV GOLDBERG

THE JERK

here was once a very coarse and unrefined Jew by the name of Moshke. Not only was he arrogant and all together not very nice, but in addition, he was simply an utter jerk!

One year, a strange desire overtook him. He wanted to be the one chosen to blow the shofar on Rosh Hashanah.

Since he was close to the poretz, the land baron, of the area, he decided to use this most powerful contact to materialize his craving. He didn't seem to care too much for the fact that usually, the most respectable and virtuous Jew of the town gets this great honor. This year, he wanted to do it himself, regardless of his questionable worthiness.

Moshke went to his friend the poretz and told him of his wish to blow the shofar in the shul on Rosh Hashanah. The poretz indifferently agreed to his friend's request, although he couldn't care less for his Jewish friend's need for this 'strange' honor of blowing a shofar.

Moshke had the poretz sign a letter which decreed that Moshke will be getting the great honor of blowing the shofar this Rosh Hashana; then, he sent the letter to the Jewish community leader.

When the community leader received the signed letter from the poretz, he was dumbfounded. He immediately went to the rabbi of the town to seek his guidance. He couldn't fathom that an arrogant imbecile like Moshke would be given the rabbi's honorable role on these most holy of days.

When the rabbi was shown the letter with the authoritative signature of the governing poretz, he just smiled and shrugged off the whole thing. He assured the community leader that all will be well, and instructed him to change nothing of the regular order of things.

When Rosh Hashanah came, Moshke came to the shul with his expensive extra-long shofar, anticipating his great moment of glory. When it was time to blow the shofar however, to his utter amazement, the holy rabbi was summoned instead of him! Surely they got the poretz's letter, he thought to himself. He justified this blunder in his mind with the assurance that tomorrow, the second day of Rosh Hashanah, he will get the honor.

When the second day came, again Moshke brought his fancy shofar and waited impatiently to be brought to the Bima, and in front of the whole community, sound his extravagant horn. To Moshke's stupendous disappointment, the rabbi was called for again to blow the shofar for the community.

"I was supposed to be the one blowing the shofar… I was supposed to be the one blowing the shofar," he kept saying to himself again and again. His rage kept growing, until his anger consumed him to such an extent that he vowed to punish the rabbi and the community leader for their blatant disrespect.

The day after Rosh Hashanah on Tzom Gedalyah, the fast of Gedalyah, the rabbi and the community leader were called to attend an emergency meeting with the poretz.

Moshke had gone to the poretz and informed him that the Jews in the Shul completely disregarded the poretz's letter, which demonstrated their disregard of his authority; the Jews, therefore, should be punished.

When confronted, the rabbi smiled and said to the poretz, "Dear sir, with all due respect, I would like to take this opportunity to teach you a little about Judaism. In the holiday season marking the beginning of the Jewish year, we blow the shofar on three different days, the first day Rosh Hashanah, second day Rosh Hashanah and on Yom Kippur. Seeing how highly regarded Moshke is in your eyes, esteemed baron, we wanted to honor him with the greatest honor, blowing shofar on Yom Kippur by Neila, the very last closing prayer."

The poretz turned to Moshke and with an irritated voice said, "Moshke, you impatient horrid little Jew. See how they wanted to honor you and you are making such a fuss over nothing! "

Moshke, with tears in his eyes, replied, "But baron, on Rosh Hashanah there are so many Tkias, blows, to make with the shofar, on Yom Kippur at Neila, there is only one blow!'

"You stupid Jew!" the poretz bellowed impatiently. "When you are given the chance, and you have the shofar in your hands, nobody can stop you, Moshke, you can make as many blows as you like!"

৪৩৩

When someone has the 'shofar' in one's hands, when a person is given the privilege of speaking in front of an audience, the individual must realize that one cannot do and say as one pleases; a person cannot make as many Tkias, blows of the shofar, as he wishes at the Neila prayer when only one is called for.

The speaker has a big responsibility, and an obligation, to say the appropriate and correct things...

THE INK OF A FARBRENGEN

There's a story told about Rabbi David Halevi Segal, known as the TaZ (the Torei Zahav), the famous commentator of the Shulchan Orech. He got married to the daughter of the famed Rabbi Yoel Sikis known as the Bach, (the Bayis Chadash), another great Shulchan Orech commentator about whom it's said that when he passed away, Gehenom was cooled down so he would pass through to Heaven without any discomfort.

To make a living, the TaZ owned a store which his wife operated while he sat and learned. After some years, she requested that he help her in the store. He would come and help for a few minutes, a quarter of an hour or maybe even half an hour, and then he would disappear, going back to his studies.

His wife, at some point, confronted him about this phenomenon, asking why he only helped her for such a small amount of time.

"Why did you marry me?" the Torah giant asked.

"Obviously I married you because you were considered an outstanding Illuy, Torah prodigy. That's why I married you." His wife answered.

"Well what is an Illuy? An Illuy is someone who can learn and master in a few minutes what it could take someone else a few hours. Well this also is the case with helping in the store, I can achieve in a few minutes more than others can in several hours!"

ജാരു

Likewise with drinking in a Farbrengen, for me, drinking a small portion of L'chaim can achieve more than what for some other people requires a whole bottle.

Dovid Hamelech, King David, says in Tehilim (45, 2), Psalms, "Leshoni Et Sofer," my tongue is like a writer's quill.

Before fountain pens and ballpoint pens were invented, people wrote with quills. Quills are writing utensils utilizing feathers that are sharpened at their ends and dipped in ink to write. The writer had to dip the quill in the ink every so often to be able to continue to write.

So it is by Farbrengens as well, we must dip our tongue is some L'Chaim to moisten it a little so the words can come out, bypassing any barriers.

(Just like without the ink it's impossible to write, without a little L'Chaim, it's difficult to bring the necessary words out on the table.)

L'Chaim Uvracha!

MORE PRECIOUS THAN PEARLS

A rabbi who was trying to recruit students for his Yeshivah, traveled to some nearby towns and villages where he met many Jewish families whose children were not given the opportunity to learn Torah.

One particularly bright boy of Bar Mitzvah age caught the rabbi's attention.

Attempting to emphasize to him the importance of learning Torah, the rabbi told him that Torah learning is more precious than pearls. The boy was quite impressed by this piece of information, and instantly enrolled in the Yeshivah.

This boy was so motivated by the rabbi's words that "learning Torah is more precious than pearls" that he learned with diligence, dedication and toiled for a whole decade!

By this time, the once simple village boy became quite a Torah scholar, having developed his mind and heart to become a fine young man of high morals, a vast knowledge of Judaism and a refined character.

The rabbi took him aside in Yeshivah one day and told him that since he now was of marriageable age, it was time that his parents make a Shidduch, marriage arrangement, for him. Therefore he should go back to his parent's village. The boy packed his belongings, and set out home bound.

On the way back to his parents, he stopped over by an inn. In the inn the boy started learning a complicated topic in Rambam which made him lose all sense of time, until he satisfactorily settled the problem almost a week later.

At the end of his stay, he informed the innkeeper that he would be leaving. The innkeeper, a simple observant Jew, presented the yeshiva student the bill which amounted to 1000 coins.

Upon seeing the bill, the student told the innkeeper he wanted to share with him what he had been laboring on for his entire sojourn in the inn.

With the innkeeper's permission, he started on an elaborate exposition.

The boy first mentioned what the Rambam had stated and then presented the Ravad's question on the Rambam. He introduced the Kesef Mishnah's answer to the Ravad's question which didn't sit well with the boy because of a few variables which he proceeded to share. Then the boy continued to explain how he managed to answer the objection of the Ravad and delivered an astounding Chidush, innovative explanation, which brilliantly settled all opinions, by taking the words of the Rambam, the Ravad and the Kesef Mishnah to a much deeper level of understanding, a beautiful tapestry of thought.

After the delivery of the inspired discourse, the boy offered the innkeeper a unique deal.

"Dear innkeeper. I have just presented to you a most complicated Kashia, complex question, with a thorough comprehension of a few commentators as well as my original solution for this intricate subject, which took me several days to learn and solve. Since you have presented me with the bill for my stay here in your cozy inn, I'd like to make you a special proposal.

"I learned from my teacher that Torah study is more precious than pearls, and here I presented you with not one pearl, but a whole necklace of pearls, strung together by an organized original Torah insight. Surely, a strand of pearls costs at least 5000 coins. You are requesting of me 1000 coins. Since Torah study is worth more than pearls, I should charge you more than 5000 coins for listening to my words of Torah; however, I will only charge you 5000 as a discount. The 1000 you ask will be settled by your debt to me, and the rest, the remaining 4000 coins, you will give to me. Surely this is a fair exchange with a great incentive for you."

Even though the innkeeper was a simple Jew who admired Torah scholars and appreciated hearing words of Torah, nevertheless he didn't agree to this 'business deal'.

"I must say that your Torah words were very moving and I've never heard such inspiring teachings. However, I need real money. I can't buy my necessities with your words," said the innkeeper.

"My dear innkeeper, I see that you drive a hard bargain. Listen, even though this is completely beneath it's worth, I will give you the privilege of having listened to my Dvar Torah, Torah insight, as even exchange for my stay's cost. My Torah presentation, which surely is more precious even than pearls, easily exceeds the worth of 5000 coins. However, I will let you have it for 1000 coins, the amount you are charging me. This is a deal of a lifetime. Have you ever heard of such a find?!" The Yeshivah scholar exclaimed in exasperation.

"I'm sorry young rabbi, but you stayed here almost a week eating three meals a day. I really need actual money!" insisted the innkeeper.

Displeased, but without any other choice, the boy took out the bag where he put the money his parents gave him, and paid his debt before turning to leave.

Proceeding on his journey, instead of going back to his parents' home, he changed his course and traveled back to his Yeshivah's rabbi.

Completely disillusioned and depressed, the boy confronted the rabbi, telling him the whole story. After he went over the entire exchange with the innkeeper, he asked him, weeping, "Rabbi, when I met you as a young boy, you told me that the words of Torah are more precious than pearls. I studied so hard, completely believing in what you had told me. Why is it that the first experience I had coming out of the Yeshivah seems to contradict your words? How come the innkeeper not only didn't respect my words of Torah as something more precious than pearls, he didn't respect them as even matching the price of pearls? In his mind, they were not even worth one fifth of the price of pearls?"

The rabbi asked his student to come to his home where he would answer his question.

The rabbi lived in a house with a barn in the back of it, as many houses had in the village. When they arrived at the rabbi's home, the rabbi asked his wife to lend him her strand of precious pearls, which she did.

The rabbi then took his disenchanted student to the barn, where his animals lived. The rabbi took the pearl necklace and proceeded to place it next to his cows head.

The cow looked at the pearls grunting and mooing in a lazy song of apathy. After sniffing them, the cow just walked away. The rabbi then took the pearls and placed them in front of the sheep. The sheep glanced at the pearls momentarily, and immediately afterwards glanced away, focusing its concentration on something more to its liking.

The rabbi continued this experiment with the rest of his livestock; however the response was the same as the cow and the sheep, disinterest and indifference.

The rabbi put the pearls away in his pocket and then took some dirty moldy hay from inside the barn and faced the animals. When the animals saw the 'treasure' in his hands, they all became very excited, making a lot of noise with each one pushing the other, to gobble the hay from the rabbi's hand.

After the rabbi let the livestock consume the hay in his hand, he walked over to his student who was watching the scene from the corner.

"My dear student, the words I told you were, and are, one hundred percent true. Torah learning is certainly more precious than pearls. However, even though pearls are really pearls it doesn't change the fact that Behemos, animals, are just Behemos!"

SEEING G-DLINESS

A great revelation of Hashem occurred during Matan Torah, the giving over of the Torah, at Har Sinai, Mount Sinai.

It says that the Jews then "saw the sounds", "Roim Es Hakolos," and that they heard that which is usually seen. Interestingly, on a deeper level these expressions also refer to physicality and spirituality. That which is only heard, something distant or concealed from eyesight which we only hear about, is likened to spirituality. Physicality and the material world are likened to that which we actually see.

On the occasion of Matan Torah, the Jews "saw the sounds," which alludes to the fact that on that day the spiritual realm which is usually hidden (Hashem), was so revealed it was palpable. It was readily seen and recognizable to the naked eye, while the physical world and its boundaries, which are usually seen and are so familiar, seemed so foreign and distant. Similar to something a person only hears about but hasn't actually seen for themselves.

In the first commandment of Aseres HaDibros, the Ten Commandments, Hashem exclaims saying "Anochi Hashem Elokecha," "I am Hashem your G-d!" Hashem revealed himself. The Jewish people clearly saw G-dliness!

But the second commandment seems like a strange put down. In the second commandment Hashem states: "Lo Yiheye Lecha Elokim Acherim Al Panai," "You shall have no other gods before me."

A logical question arises, if Hashem revealed himself to the Yidden so clearly, "I am your G-d," why then did he command them not to serve idols? Why would they want to do such a low thing when they literally saw Hashem? Seemingly the command is futile and unnecessary.

The answer to this question is quite simple. The reason the Yidden were commanded not to worship idols, even though it might appear to be beneath them, is because Hashem wanted to warn them of possible situations that could arise when they descend back into the world, after the revelation of Hashem on Har Sinai.

During this climactic time when it's visibly apparent that, "I am your G-d," this warning might seem useless, however when the Yidden will go into the world, all of a sudden they might err and give credence to the material world and its distractions.

A person could be holding onto the very highest of levels where the individual might even have the clarity of "I am Hashem your G-d," however, the world remains a place where the Yetzer Hara, the evil inclination, doesn't stop working, attempting to lure the individual to other pursuits and interests besides G-dliness, Elokim Acherim, other gods.

This idea is also reflected and reinforced in the Parsha of Naso. In the beginning and the end of the Parsha it speaks of the building of the Mishkan, the Taberacle, and the many duties and details it entails. However in the middle of it, the narrative stops and takes a tangent speaking of banishing ritually impure people from the camp and the laws of a Sota, a woman who has been promiscuous, only then to return to the Mishkan laws. Why is there a split in the Parsha and what is the connection of these apparently vastly different topics?

To answer this question let's go to the beginning of the Parsha which tells us of the tribes of the Leviim, Gershon and Merari. When the Jewish people journeyed, the Gershon family transported the Tabernacle tapestries, veils and coverings, while the Merari family carried its structural components, such as the beams, boards and pillars. They had the great privilege of dealing with the holy Mishkan on which G-d's presence dwelled. Nevertheless, Hashem is warning us that even though a person is involved in the holiest of endeavors, dealing with the Mishkan, even if the individual is someone of great distinction, he still must always be on guard. An impure person could spread contamination unto him and a person's wife could behave in an inappropriate manner, G-d forbid.

There are no guarantees.

(However, we are given some instructions and practical tips, distance yourself from impure people, and get them out of your midst. Beware of wine/ alcohol consumption because it could lead to severely improper behavior.)

Therefore, you have to watch yourself. Be aware of any impurity even when you are busy with holy things so that you can rectify them.

On a personal level, one could ask a related question. How could it be that a person who went to Yeshivah, a person who "saw G-dliness" could act in a manner below his previous level to the extent that it might even appear like Haya Kelo Haya, it's as if it never was, that it's as if he never even went to Yeshivah?

Or how could it be that even though a person learned a Ma'amer, a Chasidic discourse, or following his Davening, right afterwards, he puts the Sefer or Siddur down and can act in a manner that doesn't reflect that which was learned, or the prayer that was prayed? He then delights over a scrumptious delicious breakfast and chases after other worldly desires and interests.

How is it that a Jew who studied in Yeshivah could find himself in his office on 42nd St., or 34th St., or any street for that matter, and the billboards and streets get the person's heart pumping and mind pulsing, the material world seems so real, while G-dliness seems so very distant?

Even while a Jew is doing well spiritually and is on the level of seeing G-dliness, "I am Hashem your G-d," even if they are Bney Gershon VeMerari, the sons of Gershon and Merari involved in the holiest of work, they are still being warned, "you shall have no other gods before me," because a person should never be so assured of himself and fooled with the notion that he is unsinkable in this world. Even though one moment you are "seeing G-d," beware! The Yetzer Hara doesn't ever stop, and attempts to make the person fall with other worldly traps. The physical world, with its many faces, strongly misleads by suggesting that besides Hashem there is something else, Elokim Acherim.

The story of the Rashbi, Rabbi Shimon Bar Yochai, adds yet another dimension to this subject of "I am Hashem your G-d" and "you shall have no other gods before me."

In short: The Rashbi and his son hid in a cave for thirteen years, from the Romans, escaping a death sentence. During this time they were learning Torah day and night completely detached from the world.

Miraculously, they didn't have to worry about anything material. They had the cave for shelter. They ate from the fruit of a carob tree that grew right by the cave which also had a refreshing spring by it from which they drank. They covered their bodies with sand during the week so as not to ruin their clothes, which they only wore on Shabbos and Yomim Tovim, holidays. In this manner, completely removed from the world, they catapulted to great spiritual heights during their stay in the cave. They are renowned for their unique lofty level of awareness of "I am Hashem Your G-d" and "Ein Od Milvado," there is nothing besides Him.

When the Roman king died and their decree was annulled, twelve years after initially escaping into the cave, they exited it. They were stunned to see people dealing with plowing and planting the earth. To them it was unfathomable to waste precious time on such mundane tasks. How could people neglect Torah study and deal with worldly concerns?

Whatever they looked at was eaten by fire. A heavenly voice told them to go back into the cave saying, "Have you come out of the cave to destroy my world?" They went back for another year. When they got out of the cave this second time, they had an entirely different perspective, they recognized the great value of the Jewish people who clung to Torah and Mitzvos despite the decrees and persecution of the Romans, while working 'in the world. '

Even though the Rashbi and his son were on an extremely high state of awareness of "I am your G-d," during the extra year in the cave they developed an even deeper understanding. Despite the experience of being completely removed from the world, specifically the toil of descending into the world and working with it is essential and very important.

When they came out of the cave the second time around, the Rashbi and his son sought to help the Jewish people both physically and spiritually.

"Lasheves Yatzra," Hashem created the world in order for us to settle it. It is necessary to come out of one's 'cave' of 'seeing G-d', and help the world, all the while maintaining one's focus on G-d.

We must toil within the world (with all of its challenges, difficulties and hardships), yet, remain above it.

A vital thing to remember though is that there are two existing loves that completely contradict each other: Ahavas Hashem, love for Hashem, and Ahavas Olam, the love of the world. Each one is juxtaposed against the other, and at every moment a person has to choose between the two, "I am Hashem your G-d," Ahavas Hashem, or "other gods," Ahavas Olam...

PERSONAL MATAN TORAH

When he first came to America, the famed Chasid, Itche the Masmid was shocked at what he saw. When asked about his experiences in this new land he exclaimed, "They actually eat real hamburgers! Bepoal Mamash, in actuality!" People weren't pretending or wishing to eat hamburgers which were almost impossible to get in Europe, they were actually doing it!

Dreaming about doing something just isn't enough...

It's quite a fortuitous Hashgacha Pratis, Divine Providence, that we are gathered together on the Shabbos after Shavous, the holiday on which we celebrate receiving the Torah, celebrating the 50th year of the Hadar Hatorah Yeshivah, the world's very first Baal Teshuvah Yeshivah. It's quite a tremendous milestone for a Mosad, an institution, which has literally touched thousands of people over several generations.

We have here today alumni, who learned in the Yeshivah over four decades ago, all the way up to our current students.

The Yeshivah of Hadar Hatorah is a mother to many people... Just like with a mother who nurtures her child, so does Hadar Hatorah nurture its students, its children. Surely, at a certain point, the child wants to separate more and more from his mother, to grow independently and demonstrate how he doesn't need mommy anymore. However, no matter what happens, the child is always the mother's child. Even after the mother passes away, you are required to remember her and say Kadish.

However, remembering the past, as important as it is, shouldn't be the primary focus of an individual. "Hama'aseh Hu Haikar," the actual deed is the most important, what the person is doing now and what will they be doing in the future.

There is a Baal Teshuvah in Memphis I met a few times visiting my son-in-law's Chabad house over the years. He has kept reminding me of an analogy I gave him of doing Teshuvah, returning to one's Jewish roots or advancing in ones spirituality.

The analogy is that of driving a car. There are two things a person looks at while driving: the windshield, which shows the driver what's ahead; and the mirrors showing someone what is in back of them.

A person cannot drive properly if he is preoccupied with the mirrors showing what's behind him. Not only that, but it would be downright dangerous; but rather he needs to mostly look at what is ahead of him so he can get to his destination.

So too it is with life and with Judaism. Sometimes it's important to reflect back, but the great majority of the time, a person needs to look forward.

It's not about where you have been as much as where you are going.

Along the same line, my father used to say regarding Shidduchim: you shouldn't think of making a Shidduch, you should just make one!

G-D CENTERED

In today's day and age there is a prevalent self-centered attitude that manifests itself in many ways.

A person easily judges everything using the words "I like this" or "I don't like this."

"This part I like" while "that aspect I don't care for."

This includes this Farbrengen, "I like this Farbrengen," "I don't like this Farbrengen," "It bores me, I heard all this already" or "he is funny, it's entertaining for me, I like it!"

The pursuit of self-gratification puts all experiences on a scale measuring just how much of it is good for 'me'. The 'I' rules.

The obsession with oneself is so dominant that this self-centered attitude even permeates child rearing. Parents ask the child for what they like at every step, aiding the child to lead the way instead of being taught and shaped by the parents.

This attitude is completely the opposite of what Chassidus is all about!

This educational method completely undermines the idea of Kabalas Ole, accepting the yoke of heaven, which requires doing things that sometimes a person might not 'want' to do.

The backbone of Chasidus is Bitul HaYesh, the nullification of self, which practically means that a person doesn't just do whatever he likes when he likes it, but rather an individual is trying to fulfill the Ratzon HaElyon, the supernal will of Hashem.

A key piece of advice to rid oneself of such thinking is to get out of oneself. Stop thinking about yourself and instead of being self-centered become G-d centered.

Like it says, "Ani Nivresi Leshamesh Es Koni," "I was created to serve my maker." The only reason a person is alive is not to enjoy the world, but rather to serve Hashem.

Until a person's death, when his mission is complete, as long as a person wakes up in the morning, it means that his job isn't complete and he is needed to do more.

We must always remember that we are on a special spiritual mission, a mission which should saturate our entire time here on earth.

SIYUM HASHAS

Rabbi Vishedski remarked one time that he wanted to become a millionaire so he went to work to achieve this desire. At first he was getting $100 a week, then $200. After some time he decided to quit this ambition since it was just too difficult.

When asking him what he did then, he answered that since working to attain his first million was too hard for him, he decided to work on his second million dollars!

One of our Alumni here told me that they are about to finish learning the Shas for the second time!

There are so many people that didn't complete learning the Shas even once! Perhaps we could suggest for them to skip the first round and just jump right into learning it for the second time...

I just want to clarify and point out that the Shas isn't yours to 'finish'.

It's one thing to learn the whole cycle, but quite another to walk away from the cycle with a certain haughtiness or egotistic attitude that one has finished learning the Shas, or that one has 'completed it'.

Whether a person learns one Daf, or one Masechta, or the whole Shas, they should be conscious of the awesome fact that that they are learning and uniting with Chochmas Habore, the wisdom of the Creator.

The achievement of learning is connecting to Hashem, not to inflate one's ego as a result of learning a certain amount.

The Rebbe states in the Hayom Yom of the 29th of Teves, "Anan Po'aley DeYemama Anan," we are day workers.

The job of Chasidim is to continuously illuminating and keep working at it, adding the light of 'day', Torah & Mitzvos, to wherever we are. Unlike people who retire when they are done with work, move to Florida, and waste their days baking in the sun, Chasidim are never 'done'.

It's not up to us to 'finish' nor are we ever 'finished'; we are assigned to keep working....

Hopefully soon, we will see with our own eyes that which is "heard" (G-dliness), and hear about that which is "seen" (physicality) in the coming of Mashiach in the Geula Hashlema, the complete redemption, when Hashem will be completely revealed.

ൟരඝ

From a Farbrengen celebration of Hadar Hatorah Yeshivah's 50th Anniversary, Shabbos Naso, 5772

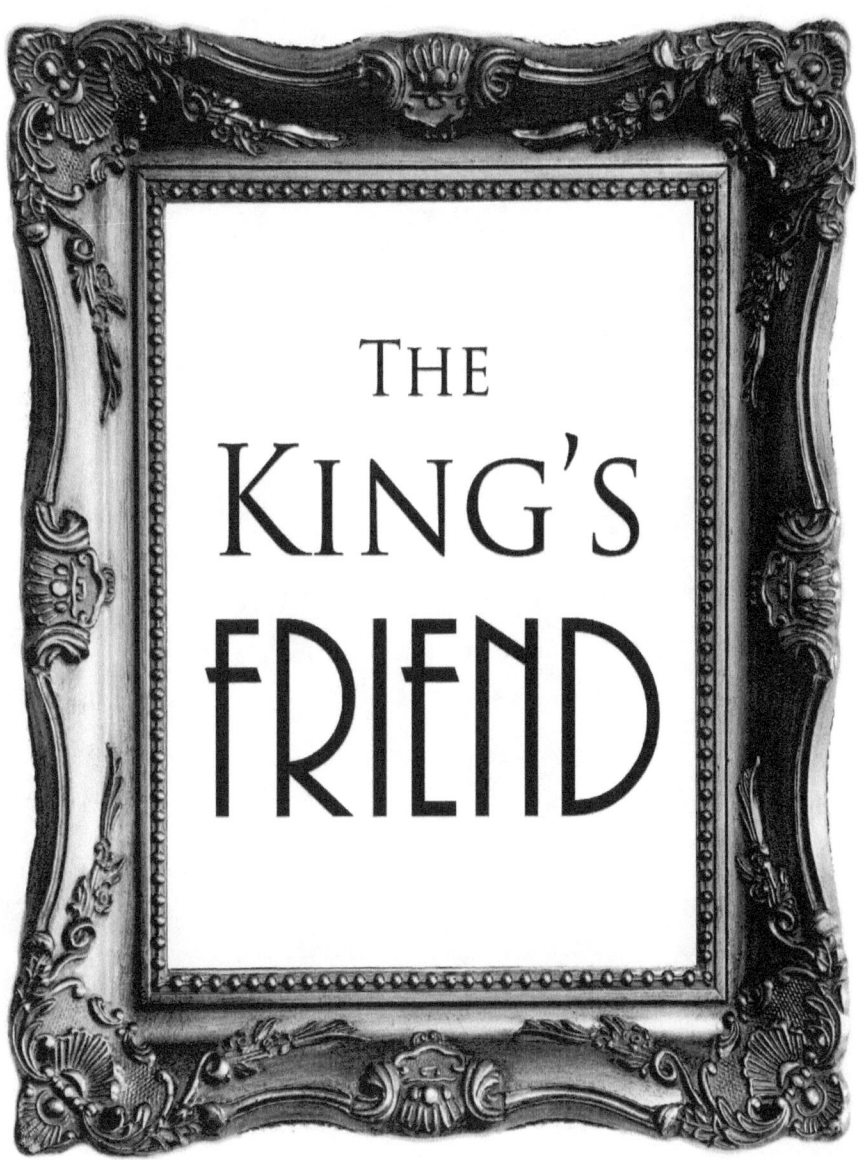

THE
KING'S
FRIEND

BASED ON AN URBAN LEGEND

nce there lived a gentile king who delighted in having an audience with a particular rabbi who lived in the kingdom's capital. The two would converse on various subjects, and the rabbi's acuity and sharp intellect amazed the king again and again. No one could compare in counsel and wisdom to the charming rabbi.

The king had a fascination with outings to the country where he would invite the rabbi so they could discuss specifically the kingdom's happenings and latest news.

The rabbi had a way of always weaving into the conversation the idea of Hashgacha Pratis, Divine Providence, constantly seeking to connect the unfolding events with Hashem's underlying presence and guiding hand.

One time, on one of these outings, the king decided to go hunting. Accompanied by the rabbi, his companion of choice, the king insisted that the rabbi also hunt together with him.

Unfamiliar with the sport, the rabbi fumbled with the rifle and accidentally, a shot escaped from the weapon. A bitter scream pierced the forest, a scream from none other than the king himself! The rabbi had mistakenly shot the king, damaging his hand forever by shooting off one of his fingers.

Enraged, the bleeding king had his guards imprison the rabbi immediately with swift orders to put him into one of the dungeon's prison chambers.

Months passed, and the king's injury slowly healed. His hand was getting stronger, and his desire to go on one of his outings finally made him plan a most extravagant trip to many far-off lands.

In one particularly exotic location, the king was warned not to leave the camp grounds because of many hostile natives lurking about. However, the king's adventurous spirit was sparked by the idea of seeing the area as it was, going off the beaten path.

Throughout the trips he missed the wisdom and friendship of the brilliant rabbi. If only he was there now, he would accompany him and share deep insights into these experiences...

As he was exploring alone, he was captured by cannibal tribesmen. As was their custom, they inspected their captured 'merchandise' before cooking. They were alarmed to find that the enticing specimen before them had a missing finger. Immediately they declared it a bad omen, and discarded the king close to his campgrounds.

The king was beside himself with joy. The rabbi's 'blunder' saved his life.

He immediately changed course and redirected his entourage to go back home. He had to speak to the rabbi.

After much traveling, when they finally arrived at the capital, the king immediately set the rabbi free.

As he related the events that transpired, the king exclaimed, "Dear rabbi, you have always spoken of Divine Providence and how everything comes down from heaven for our good, and I see that here... The events that happened to me on my journey clearly display revealed Divine Providence. But rabbi, I have one question to pose to you. What was the Divine Providence as it relates to you? You were in the dungeon for months; where is the good in that?"

The rabbi smiled as he answered, "Your majesty, the Divine Providence in my predicament is just as clear as it is in your experience, why, if I wasn't in the dungeon, I would have been with you, and the cannibals would have eaten me, G-d forbid."

"What lesson could we take from all this?" asked the king.

After a little thought the rabbi answered.

"Perhaps the general lesson is that everyone is essentially a friend of the ultimate king, the creator of heaven and earth. Since He is a true and good friend who wants the very best for us, we therefore must always have faith that all experiences are really for the best.

More particularly we could look at our personal experiences now... A seemingly horrible event could reveal itself later as a lifesaver. In addition, even if a person is in an undesirable place where they feel trapped, that also contains good. Who knows what cannibals are outside the situation which the very 'prison' is saving the individual from..."

ಕಾಲ

THE ART
OF
HUGGING
A TREE

A GIMMEL TAMMUZ DIARY

here is she? I lift my eyes searching.

The silhouettes cast on the white hanging sheet catch my eye. Back lit by the sun, their shadows create the most intriguing visual. Unlike a painting or a photograph this sight is alive…

The profile of the faces of women clearly defined on the stretched white sheet is gently waving in the breeze. Old and young ladies' lips are moving in prayer while the Psalms held in their hands are close to their heads. The outlines of restless children are moving about as much as they can in the packed line. The baby strollers' presence is revealed by the shape of the handles.

If there was to be a flag for this place and state of being this would be it, anonymous contours of people praying.

This stretched hanging white sheet, the Mechitza, separating the men's line from the woman's line, with its shadows, could be a piece in some Jewish life museum.

I can't seem to find them. I return my attention back to the prayer book in my hand and continue to utter the words in a whisper.

They are probably far ahead, maybe they went in already?

Hopefully the woman's line is faster than the man's line which just doesn't seem to proceed.

ഇറ

Here we are at the Rebbe's resting place, which is anything but restful. Especially today, Gimmel Tammuz, the third day of the month of Tammuz, the anniversary of the Rebbe's passing, his Yahrtzeit.

This place is buzzing. The cars parked in every area possible make it difficult for the waves of new cars coming in to find a place to park. People are everywhere, on the sidewalk, in the guest lobby areas for men and those for woman, and of course the massive lines to the Rebbe's Ohel.

The commotion of people creates a happening atmosphere of longing and also that of desperation...

In addition to just be there on this auspicious day, everyone has come for a private reason, a need for a personal redemption in some realm. Some come for a spiritual helping hand in the betterment of their financial situation while some seek blessings for improved health. Some come to pray for finding a mate while some for salvation; for having a baby, etc.

The sheer amount of people present is quite impressive.

My goodness, this rabbi touches so many people, I can't help thinking to myself. It's striking no matter how many times I see it.

The lines are long and packed. Everybody is waiting for their turn to come into the Rebbe's resting place for the allotted and strictly enforced two minutes on this special day, Gimmel Tammuz.

Before joining the long lines I had gone to the restroom. My wife, meanwhile, took the kids with her in the woman's line.

When I returned I saw they advanced too far for me to offer to take a kid and elevate some burden from my wife, now with all of our four kids, whose ages are four and under.

I'm reading the Maaneh Lashon, a compilation of prayers and Psalms recited at the proximity of the burial sites of Tzadikim, which I picked up from the table by the candle lighting stand.

Just like everybody else here, I've got so many Brachos, blessings, to ask for my family and I.

Half an hour goes by, and then another and then yet another before suddenly familiar voices awaken me from my meditative state induced by reciting the holy words while I shuckle back and forth.

Finally! Amongst the sea of people swaying and waiting in prayer, I'm relieved and happy to see my family.

The kids bounce back and forth between my wife and me until we each take two.

Before we go forward, each in our own line, we take off our children's leather shoes ahead of time, as it is customary not to wear leather shoes in a holy place, such as this one, where the Rebbe is buried.

I'm holding our nine month old daughter and one of our twin girls who are four. The other twin and our two year old son are with my wife in the woman's line. It seems We are now so close to enter.

The woman's line proceeds ahead taking my wife and the two kids a bit forward and soon out of sight.

My baby daughter is busy leafing through various prayer books I gave her while I balance my four year old girl on the fence dividing the men and woman's line all the while reciting Psalms and then my own P'an, personal letter to the Rebbe. I figure it's better to read it now in the line since the Ohel will be too squashed for me to endure a minute or two inside with the two kids in my care.

Approximately half an hour goes by.

Finally, as we are almost by the front of the line, my four year old shocks me. At first it didn't register because I was dumbfounded so I asked her to repeat herself.

"Abba I have to make." She informs me.

Perfect timing! Just as we are about to enter the Ohel after nearly two hours in line… Oy!

I take her hand and push aside the few people in front of me with several excuse me's. The guard looks at me as I try to pass through and I tell him I have to take my daughter to the potty.

We run into the loaded lobby area that is just brewing with life. We make our way through several Minyanim, quorums, praying the afternoon prayer, Mincha.

Ironically enough, my high wishes and noble prayers are reduced in a matter of seconds to a desperate plea, "Hashem, please help her keep it in until we reach the toilet... Please save us from an accident in the middle of one of these packed Minyanim!"

We make it to the bathroom, thank G-d, after which we wash our hands and run back to the line explaining to every guard on our way, very apologetically, that the young lady had to go potty.

We are allowed to go to the front of the line and are let in.

I swoop up my 'older' daughter with my left arm while my right arm is clutching my baby.

I somehow manage to knock on the door and enter with both of our kids in my arms.

The Ohel is full to capacity.

I give my big four year old girl my P'an to rip up and throw into the Ohel.

She takes the picture of flowers she made and brought especially for the Rebbe and puts them in.

Instead of reading the entire P'an there's only one request that comes to mind that seems to encapsulate it all. I call out together with my daughters, "Mashiach Now!" These simple two words pack a mighty punch, demanding, asking, wishing, praying that the righteous redeemer of Israel will come immediately ushering in the complete and final redemption.

It seems also to be the perfect request in this auspicious occasion celebrating the Rebbe, since the Rebbe's life's work centered on making Mashiach a reality. That would definitely be the perfect elixir for all of us here and the world over.

We leave the Ohel as we are facing the Rebbe's stone. I'm walking backwards out of respect.

We walk out searching for my shoes which were moved next to a pile of dozens of other shoes. While I'm putting on my shoes I can't help but think, "We made it!"

The setting sun is shining a golden light on this holy scene. I briefly look back. The lines are still packed. The frenzy continues even though the day is about to depart. The breeze is blowing gently, somehow managing to let the heat linger.

As we walk back to the lobby area I'm taken aback as I see it. Maybe it never looked like this ever before. Perhaps it never will grow this way ever again. Even though I thought I saw it many times before, I didn't really see it, until this past Shabbos.

.

৪৩৫৩

This past Shabbos I was by the Ohel together with a couple of thousand other people.

Rabbis, Chasidim, students and guests from the world over gathered there for a Shabbos of unity and Farbrengens, Chasidic gatherings, as preparation for Gimmel Tammuz.

All who came were treated to free lodging and festive meals that reeked of plenty.

Farbrenging together, learning together, eating together and celebrating together made it a truly outstanding spiritual Shabbos experience of togetherness.

The enormous newly built halls of the lobby area were filled with hundreds of tables and benches, all needless to say, packed with guests.

Looking around, wherever I was, amazed me, since the sheer numbers of people created a Chasidic landscape scene, Chasidim as far as the eye can see.

At one Farbrengen I happened to be in, a charismatic rabbi from Israel kept those in attendance riveted for literally hours. His stories and powerful Torah teachings from the Rebbe were given over with great energy and brilliance. The mood was enhanced further with moving Nigunim, Chasidic melodies, and delicious served delicacies (that were complementary).

During one of the Nigunim I happened to look around. Right above the table we were situated by, there was a big window. This window was a perfect frame for this 'postcard picture' I saw.

Through the window you could see the sight of this grandiose tree in the foreground, while in the background white clouds were swimming in the light blue sky.

Its big trunk loomed over the cemetery scene. Its unusual branches, which were quite big and trunk like, aimed at the sky, made this tall tree look like a giant human figure with outstretched arms towards the heavens above.

Wow!

I looked around me at the masses of people present and then I looked back at the tree.

Making it even more intriguing was the fact that this tree was covered with vines of ivy. The ivy surrounded the trunk completely and went all the way up to those big branches. This big tree was fully dressed with ivy head to toe. How interesting...

This was a cemetery after all. The stones were quiet and gray. The land was flat.

In this solemn place, to see this unique beautiful tree, a burst of life, was somehow not a contradiction, even though it really stood out.

I then noticed the bottom of the window, through which you could see a bit of the ivy growing on a fence which surrounds the cemetery.

The ivy on the fence reached maybe six feet while the ivy on the tree reached thirty or forty feet tall.

I glanced back at the people at the Farbrengen. Then I stretched my gaze towards the other Farbrengens in the distance.

I looked through the window again, and this time, a connection just clicked.

The view of this magnificent tree was a metaphoric mirror of what this majestic gathering was all about.

All of us are the ivy, connected to the stately tree, the Rebbe.

The tree is very tall. The ivy is enabled to grow tall too, because of its connection to the tree. All those here have come in honor of the Rebbe, the spiritual leader of the generation, are clinging to the tall tree; we are cleaving to the Rebbe. We are all, therefore, climbing upwards, heaven bound.

Because the tree is so high, reaching with its thick trunk like branches outstretched to the firmament, the ivy is also able to reach up high, in a sense, touching the sky.

Because of our connection to this grand supporting fatherly figure, who was constantly extended to heavenly matters, we are able to reach higher levels than we could have reached utilizing any other way, and truly touch heaven.

He is a lofty tree connected with the Torah, the tree of life, in a seamless bond. By attaching ourselves to him we attach to that which he is attached to...

૪୦୯ଷ

All of the sudden, after these flashing thoughts from Shabbos, I glance back towards those lines. Now inspired by my Shabbos epiphany, the seemingly unending lines of people start resembling long vines of ivy, every face a leaf.

We walk towards our van, where my wife waits for us with the other two children.

After feeding the kids and ourselves (I fasted this whole day), we prepare for the ride home. The intensity of the day impregnates with inspiration.

I start up our van and begin the drive home hoping, expecting, revealed goodness.

The sun's setting rays of light cast an enchanting glow that suggests that this day isn't really over...

Today reignites something that will burn within all of us who come to the Rebbe, and those of us who let the Rebbe's teachings come into our lives, transforming, elevating and literally catapulting us sky high.

૪୦୯ଷ

Ohel Chabad Lubavitch at the Rebbe's Ohel is located at: 226-20 Francis Lewis Blvd. Cambria Heights, New York 11411 Tel 718 723 4545 www.OhelChabad.Org

૪୦୯ଷ

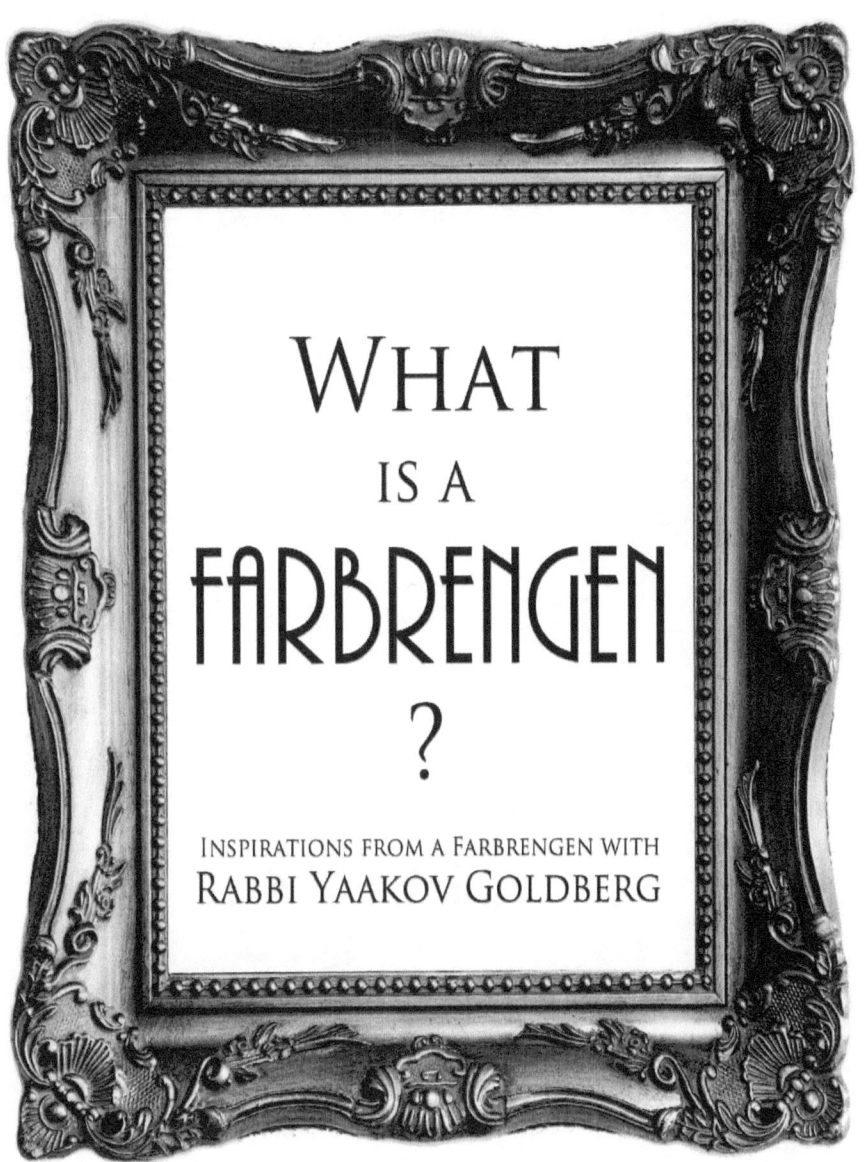

WHAT
IS A
FARBRENGEN
?

INSPIRATIONS FROM A FARBRENGEN WITH
RABBI YAAKOV GOLDBERG

he speaker successfully managed to lose his entire audience with his well prepared speech. Some people were sleeping, some were clearly daydreaming, and some were just uninterested. All except for one individual who was paying close attention to every word.

He wasn't just passively listening. Oh no. He was nodding his head up and down in agreement at times, and sometimes he was shaking his head left to right in disagreement. This phenomenon excited the speaker to such an extent he continued his speech inspired solely by his avid listener, his only listener.

After the speech, the speaker went to this listener and thanked him for listening to him so carefully. Without his attention, he admitted, he would have stopped the speech long ago. However, he was wondering, what was the shaking of the head all about?

The lone listener from the audience told him, "I think you misunderstood me. Let me tell you what happened... I'm a shepherd. I watch and take care of my goats. Last week I lost one of my goats. I looked everywhere for this goat but I couldn't find it, nevertheless, I decided I won't give up so easily. Then, I saw an ad publicizing a speech by you, so I decided to come and maybe I'll find my goat here. Strangely enough, as you started speaking, I was struck by your appearance. You looked like my goat! I was so happy. However I was thinking to myself, wait, I can't be so hasty, I have been looking for a while now for my goat, I have to make sure. I studied your face and I thought to myself that yes, you are my goat, so I shook my head up and down, but then I would think again, no, you're not my goat, so I shook my head from left to right... So this went on throughout your entire lecture, until you finished, which is when I made my final decision... You definitely are a goat! But, you are not my goat!"

What is a Farbrengen? A Farbrengen is not a speech!

What is a speech? A speech, more often than not, is an exercise in disinterest. The speaker, usually, isn't truly interested in what he is saying and neither are the people present. Why? It's very simple.

The hearts of the people that are supposed to be listening aren't into it since the heart of the speaker isn't into what he is saying. After the speech, 'Lo Paga, VeLo Naga', 'it didn't hit and didn't touch'.

The words, needless to say, didn't affect the listeners or even touch them in the slightest.

A Farbrengen isn't a prepared event. It's not about thinking of what to say, it's about what comes out of your heart.

There's an interesting old Chasidic saying that encapsulates this notion of how Chasidim loath speeches. It's a play of some P'sukim, verses, which describe a situation of a Jew who is found to be worshipping idols, the punishment of which is to be stoned to death.

"When you are told and you realize (that such an event has happened, that a Jew actually worshipped Idols), you are to inquire thoroughly. If in fact the report is authenticated and accurate - Nachon Hadavar- (then) this is an abomination that was committed within Israel." (Shoftim 17:4)

The saying goes like this: If you are told and you inquired thoroughly, and it is true, 'Nachon Hadavar', that the talks in the Farbrengen were prepared, 'Muchan Hadavar', then this truly is an abomination that has transpired in Israel!

(The word play is off of the verses words Nachon Hadavar, which means that 'it is accurate', however the word Nachon is close in spelling and root to the word Muchan which means prepared.)

The Rebbe Rashab would pray before a Farbrengen that the words he says will inspire both him and the listeners.

୨୦୦୧

Why are we repeating the same stories everybody knows again and again? Especially now, everything is in English, you probably heard almost everything already, if not in Hebrew or Yiddish then in English, so what's the point?

Like Yetzias Mitzraim, the exodus from Egypt, every year there is a Mitzvah to retell the story, so it is on 19th Kislev and every other auspicious time.

Sippur, the word story in Hebrew, comes from the word Sapir, sapphire - a shiny gem. This alludes to the act of making something shine, which refers to make revealed, to illuminate. We retell the stories that we all know to *continue* to shed light and to illuminate this very time we find ourselves in.

Like everything else, there is a certain Seder, an order, in a Farbrengen, in which one speaks and others listen. Even though sometimes it could be very hard to listen, nevertheless Halacha states that, 'HaShomea KeOmer Dami', 'the one that hears is like the one that speaks', so really everybody is speaking in a Farbrengen...

Interestingly enough, Hafatza and Shlichus aren't just about somebody else; you have to start with yourself, 'Mibsarcha Al Tisalem', 'don't ignore your own flesh.'

The Rashbatz was the Melamed of the Frierdiker Rebbe when he was a young boy. The Rashbatz also used to help put him to sleep at night. By the nighttime Krias Shema, he taught the young Rebbe to-be to declare and resolve that what was, was, but *tomorrow it has to be completely different.*

No matter what today's accomplishments were, no matter what happened yesterday, tomorrow IT HAS TO BE, radically different, better!

༄ఆ

How could someone proclaim that 'I'm a Jew in my heart' yet not want to touch a Mitzvah or learn Torah? How could that come to be?

There's a story of the two Masmidim, great scholars, who lived in a certain town. One scholar used to hunch over his Gemara for so many years he was affectionately called 'the hunchback', the other used to sit on a log and learn for around 18 hours a day for many years to the extent that he created a groove in the log he used to sit on.

In the same town lived a grocery store owner who only used to come to Shul on Rosh Hashanah and Yom Kippur.

One time, someone came up to the scholar who sat on a log studying, and jokingly asked him why doesn't he cut back on his learning a little. Instead of learning for 18 hours a day, since he already learned so much for so many years, he could take it easy now in his old age and learn just seventeen or sixteen hours a day.

The rabbi got very serious and exclaimed that all Jews are interconnected. If he, G-d forbid, decreased his learning even one hour there will be a domino effect, a downward spiral affecting other Jews holding at lower levels of learning then him, and then, G-d forbid, the town's grocer will lose whatever connection he has to Judaism and he won't even come to Shul on Yom Kippur!

There was a guy who used to Daven really quickly. One time, he Davened a 'Hodu/ Aleinu Davening'. He said Hodu and Aleinu and not much in between. As he came home, his wife asked him why he came so soon from Shul. In his defense he said he doesn't know what she means since he Davened from Hodu to Alenu.

Later on, at night, he came home hungry expecting a delicious meal. His wife was on to him, and she wanted to teach him a lesson. She brought out a fish head, and a fish tail, without anything in between, and placed the plate right in front of her fast Davening husband. The dinner and message were served.

When a person makes an internal gap, thinking this is how I am during Davening or learning Torah and this is me at business, he becomes like a split personality. You can't even recognize the person at work as the same one Davening for an hour or studying Torah for an hour etc.

This kind of split personality behavior on whatever level, affects a Yid on a lower level of observance. So much so that it creates a reality where there could be a Jew to whom it suffices to be just Jewish in their heart without having it manifest in DOING a mitzvah or learning Torah.

ജ്ഞ

When going to the Mikvah even though you are completely submerged except for one hair, the Halacha is that the T'vila, submersion, doesn't count! The person has to be completely 100% under the water, immersed in it. The fact that he has even one hair above water proves that he has thoughts somewhere else, he isn't completely 'there'.

In learning Torah, Davening and just everyday living of a Torah life, a person has to be completely immersed, completely drenched in it. Otherwise, its proof he isn't really fully there. It's absolutely *not* about Davening quickly, while keeping the phone on, so you can speak to someone else, with 'very important' business or social matters…

Nine months before going into the prison we find ourselves in, the Rebbe requested and demanded from all of us to '*DO ALL YOU CAN TO BRING MASHIACH!*'

We simply have to accept all that has been given to us, and just complete the job.

If you look at the first Maamar of the Rebbe he clearly declared his mission, to bring Mashiach. He tried in every which way, through sending Shluchim all over the world, saying Sichos and Ma'amarim dedicated to this goal, unlike any other Rebbe in history. He wanted to actualize and manifest all of the Rebbeim's work by bringing Mashiach and the Geula Hashlemah, the complete redemption.

There was a Chasid of the Alter Rebbe who had a dream while his Rebbe was in prison. He dreamt that the Maggid of Mezritch was at the head of a table surrounded by great Tzadikim, and the Maggid was distressed, saying to the Tzadikim present that his favorite Talmid is in trouble, he is in prison and Chasidus itself is in danger.

Immediately the Rashbi created a Beis Din, a court of Jewish law, and they ruled that the Alter Rebbe should be set free. Since he started revealing Chasidus in the revolutionary way of comprehending the inner aspects of Torah with the Chochmah, Binah and Daas (intellect, understanding and knowledge) of person, when he leaves prison he should spread it even more than before; and that Chasidim should and will always have the upper hand.

When the Chasid awoke, he realized that this dream was no simple dream. That day the Alter Rebbe was set free...

Even though it's difficult to say, this story very easily connects with our time now where we unfortunately don't hear the Rebbe say Ma'amarim or Sichos, we don't see the Rebbe give dollars etc. 'The Rebbe is in prison'. However there was a Psak Din, a Halachic ruling, that the Rebbe will be set free and Chasidus will be spread out much more than before. Just like with the Alter Rebbe whose writings and Hafatza of Chasidus Chabad, after the 19th Kislev redemption, dramatically increased in multiple ways.

The Alter Rebbe was in prison for 53 days, corresponding to the 53 chapters of the Tanya. It was said that it was a Mesiras Nefesh for him to be imprisoned, but why?

The Alter Rebbe's whole Etzem, essence, was to spread Chasidus, and in prison he could not. For someone like himself whose whole life was Chasidus, and living out the Baal Shem Tov's vision of spreading Chasidus outwards, therefore hastening the coming of Mashiach, and not being able to do that, is very painful, it's Mesiras Nefesh.

ഇറ

Who did the Alter Rebbe write the Tanya for?

The Alter Rebbe wrote the Tanya because there were thousands of Chasidim needing guidance and there was a limitation of time. He said he wrote it for people he knew, to answer their questions.

Why are the people that are here in Lubavitch here? There are thousands of people that were not in Lubavitch Yeshivahs or knew of the Rebbe.

However, all those who are Shayach, akin to, the Alter Rebbe, 'he saw' and 'he knew' beforehand. He 'knew me' and he 'knew you'. And he foresaw that this Tanya is the prescription for our problems....

The Chasidim when they first came about had no name, but people used to call them the Freileche Chevre, the happy folk.

Nevertheless the Alter Rebbe dedicated three chapters of the Tanya about Atzvos, sadness, chapters 26, 27, and 28. The Alter Rebbe debated with himself regarding the inclusion of one letter in a word in the Tanya, the Vav in Vechulu or just leave it without the Vav, Chulu, for several weeks... Only over the inclusion of one letter in a word! However he wrote 3 whole chapters about sadness. Why?

Because, *no Avera*, transgression, could lead a person to so much damage as sadness.

The Rebbe said the 'Makas Hamedina', the plague of the nation, is sadness. Driving many people to be addicted to therapists... A person has to be happy, not Hololus, frivolousness, but real Simcha.

The Lashon, description, said about the 19th of Kislev, which 'gave' us Chasidus, is that it gives Chayus, liveliness. Chayus in Avodas Hashem is more than just important, it's vital, like the difference between a living body and the opposite. When a person does a Mitzvah they should be really excited about it, not excited to get it over with.

People essentially want two things, truth and life. Imagine the following scenario: A person is offered that whatever he wishes for will be granted on the condition that he shall be put into a coma state, and through injections, his fantasy life will be fulfilled. What would you answer such a proposition?

Surely, no one wants such a thing. People want life, real life, and truth, not make believe, real truth. Chassidus, brings life, Chayus, to Avodas Hashem, and of course it's the completeness of truth, the truth in its entirety - Torah T'mima, the complete Torah, both Nigla, the revealed, and Nistar, the hidden.

Life can be difficult, with many matters that require our attention.

However it's very important not to get confused, and we must materialize what the Rebbe, and the previous Rebbeim, have entrusted to us *within our everyday life. Don't lose focus!*

Let's immerse ourselves completely into Torah as it is illuminated by its inner light, Chasidus and Darchey HaChasidus, the ways of Chasidus.

Hopefully today will be the auspicious day that the Rebbe will come out of this prison that is Galus, exile, together with all of us, and we will be set free in the complete redemption with the coming of Mashiach now.

৪৩৫৪

OUR PURIM POGROM

I wasn't planning to write about this since I initially figured this was solely a private matter. After replaying it in my mind and talking about it with friends and family, I realized that it should be shared with others too, since it wasn't about my family and me personally, but rather it happened to us because we are Jewish, making it relevant to any Jew.

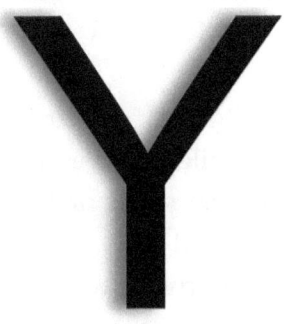esterday was Purim, on which we drove all around Crown Heights, our neighborhood, delivering Shaloch Manos, gifts of food, for several hours. Our kids, needless to say, were restless and exhausted from the long 'ride', even though they had many fun stops at their teachers and several family friends.

However today, Shushan Purim, the ride is to New Jersey, to spend Shabbos with family, which is long for an entirely different reason.

The 45 minutes it should have taken us, are stretching out mercilessly because of the severely congested traffic.

"Why aren't we moving?" is becoming the common complaint that not only our children are voicing but we too, their parents.

This is Erev Shabbos after all, and we have to get there before Shabbos.

Meanwhile, the music is playing Pesach songs from the Seder night, and the Shaloch Manos from yesterday are being consumed in a rare exhibit of health watch abandon. Purim is just once a year after all, and in just a couple of hours, even Shushan Purim will go on a yearlong vacation.

As we sing 'Ma Nishtana', 'Dayenu' and other Seder hits, psychologically at least, Purim is over and Pesach is next.

We cross the Manhattan Bridge towards Manhattan, leaving Brooklyn behind, while the Pesach music just gets us more and more into the spirit of the exodus from Egypt and the splitting of the Red sea.

When we finally cross the river, we are disappointed to find that the Canal Street entrance is blocked off. We usually take Canal to the West Side Highway up to the George Washington Bridge into New Jersey.

We are trying to get onto Canal Street; however, the small streets just don't seem to let us.

When we need to make a right turn to get onto Canal St., we see 'no right turn' signs, and when we need to make a left turn to get on Canal St., we see 'no left turn' signs.

All other alternatives to get to the West Side highway are equally clogged and hopeless. If only we could somehow get on Canal.

I never before saw Manhattan's traffic so slow; we are literally inching our way forward very very slowly in half circles.

With every car flow allowance, the traffic is being directed by the police, it seems like only a few cars are allowed to go and then the police stop the rest of the cars in a futile endless manner that keeps us from moving on our way.

I can't help but beep my horn inspired by my constant time checks.

Whereas the kids are just anxious, we, the parents, are concerned if we will make it to our destination. Making Shabbos on leftover Shaloch Manos on the side of the road doesn't seem so appealing...

Oy Vey! It's already 5pm. Had it not been for this stagnant traffic, we would have been at our hosts by now. We call our N.J. family who calm our fears and promise us that surely we will make it since we have just enough time.

Looking at the stuck streets doesn't help inspire me much; however, I keep trying, not knowing what lies ahead for us.

After going in and out of Canal Street in a high frequency wave like manner, through both SoHo and the Tribeca streets, we are getting closer. On a very busy 6th avenue, driving north we approach Canal St. yet again.

Oh, Canal St. Oh! I see you.

Yes, finally we will make it. My hope resurrected, I near Canal as slow as a snail on wheels.

As we finally get to Canal we are greeted by a 'no left turn' sign!

Oh no, another half circle ahead, I think to myself as we just pass Canal and are stopped by the traffic just past it on 6th avenue.

The upscale SoHo neighborhood impresses with its beautiful tall buildings all around us.

We are in the middle lane. The left lane is reserved for buses, and is currently empty. To the left of us is a triangular street island in the middle of which is a police van. On the sidewalk of the island, just by us, there are about fifteen teenagers hanging out. This group of kids is made up of both boys and girls. As we are sandwiched between the cars in front and behind us, I hear something thrown onto our car from the left side, a pebble perhaps.

I look at the teenagers who are looking right back at me. I lower the window against my wife's advice and calmly ask, "Why would you do something like that?"

A girl from the group stoically looks at me coldly. "Huh. Just move on. Yeah, just get going." She hisses while staring me down.

"Close the window. Close it right now!" my wife demands of me. I close it, and then I look at her while shrugging my shoulders.

All of a sudden, taken by complete surprise, a smashing sound shocks our family. The sound of breaking glass is followed by a blend of children crying hysterically and my horn blowing. I sound the horn on the car to call attention to the area and ward off these 'all American' teenagers.

The rear window of our van was smashed with a big hole in the center of it. It looks like they threw a rock, a big rock.

This window is situated right behind me, the driver. This window is adjacent to our **two** month old baby's car seat, with him inside it.

Immediately after the blowing of the horn I go to the back of the car and inspect our baby. He is covered with broken glass and as I remove him from the car seat pieces of glass fall off of him.

The only exposed part of his body is his face, but thank G-d, he isn't bleeding, and he isn't harmed, miraculously. After removing a piece of glass close to his eye, I give him to my wife to hold while I check our other children, who are all in the van with us, hysterical.

My kids in the backseat are crying and talking at the same time. The most alarming comment I hear is, "My face. I felt glass bounce off of my face."

I inspect each kids face for any harm and again, with each one, I thank G-d that they are physically ok, as far as I can tell.

I jump out of the van and run towards the parked police van, which is only about twenty feet from our van this whole time. I'm yelling at the top of my lungs, "These people just threw a rock at our car," I point to the fleeing kids who aren't even running, they are coolly walking away from the scene.

To my utter amazement, besides the fact that the police didn't come to the scene as they heard the big crashing window, the police officer didn't even get out of his vehicle. He had his door open and just had one leg out. I repeated my scream loudly, but nevertheless he didn't budge.

From behind me, my wife, clutching our baby approaches them, getting closer than I am, and yells at them to catch the kids, who under the police's nose, just threw a rock, smashing the window next to a newborn baby.

Some people around ask about the welfare of the baby. Some bystanders advise me to get the van number of the police so I could complain about them.

The kids are freaking out while the emotions of both my wife and I are running high.

Meanwhile, the police officers catch the group.

The time is ticking, and Shabbos is getting closer and closer. Completely (thankfully) ignorant of any police protocol, I explain to the officer that our Sabbath is coming and we must be on our way. The lady police officer convinces me to identify the perpetrator. She insists it'll only be a moment and that it's important that I do so.

I walk with her explaining I didn't see exactly who threw the rock. "Just come for one minute," she persists.

The male officer has the group cornered by the underground subway station, between the teller and the wall. Quite a few heads keep turning at the sight of this occurrence.

As I approach them, some of the groups faces express an unspoken feeling of, "Oh no, here he is."

The cop asks me to identify the perpetrator.

I tell him the truth, "I didn't see exactly who smashed the window. But this is the girl that I had the word exchange with." I said as I pointed the girl out. She was wearing a distinct blue scarf.

"Without you seeing who did it I can't arrest anyone," the cop said. "But, I will get their information," he states.

I ask for his name but he doesn't have any papers to write on. The police papers on him he can't give me he says.

Time is of the essence. Shabbos is nearing and we must go.

As I walk briskly back to the car I converse with the lady police officer and get her name which she writes on some slip of paper I find in my wallet. At one point, as I tell her what happened, she just exclaims, "These kids are just animals!"

As we prepare to rush out, it occurs to me to ask my children if they saw who threw the rock.

One of my daughters, through the tears, says the same girl that spoke back to me said, "I'm going to smash the Jew's car." It was that girl she said.

As the second police officer joins us by our van I tell him that my daughter saw who it was.

"It was the girl with the blue scarf," I tell him.

"There were two girls with a blue scarf", he answers me. I only saw one.

'There were only three girls in the group, can't we call them back some other time and I'll identify her?" I ask.

"There were five girls and it would be incredibly difficult to actually get someone arrested at a later date," he retorts with an attempted sincere sly smile.

I get a feeling that he is trying to brush this incident under the rug.

He continues to talk about the futility of pursuing this incident as he sympathizes with us, saying that even the insurance will not cover the window, but I don't trust him.

The lady cop just looks down while the male officer smooth talks us.

"This is horrible. I've got kids these ages too you know," he says.

"Are you going to file a complaint or something?" I ask.

"I could file a report, but that would take a few minutes..." He replies.

"No, we have to run, the Sabbath is coming..." I answer.

"Maybe you could give me your name since you have the names of the group you actually caught," I ask.

"It won't matter if you get my name. You won't be filing a report with me," he quickly answers.

His answer seems strange to me, making no sense, since he has the info of the teens, it seems most appropriate to link that to the report I will make, or perhaps later some investigation could take place based on the names and numbers he collected.

The nice demeanor of the officer doesn't offer any solace since he is insinuating from various angles, shockingly, that nothing will be done to reprimand these teens, not even talk to their parents about what happened.

"You have ten days to file a report sir," the cop tells me before we go. "It's the first precinct, just a couple of blocks from here."

"Maybe you should put the baby back in the car seat," the cop suggests.

I look at the baby seat covered with glass, the broken window with the gaping hole in the middle of it looming just inches away, threatening to break further.

"I don't think that's a good idea," I quip back.

I give the baby to one of the girls to hold momentarily, before my wife moves to the back of the vehicle and shields the backseat from the window by placing a jacket in between.

The intensity of these moments creates a mood so thick with emotion it is almost palpable. (This feeling stays with us for the next couple of days.)

The kids are whimpering still, as we leave Canal and Sixth Avenue, trying to escape SoHo.

Our hosts call us and we explain to them that unfortunately, we will not be able to make it to New Jersey this Shabbos.

Maybe we should go to some Shluchim in Manhattan, they suggest. The deadlock in traffic in the area discourages any such idea. We are heading back to Brooklyn.

It's around 5:30 pm now. Candle lighting time is around 5:38pm. The pressure is on.

We are making our way back through the fancy streets of SoHo not unnoticed.

"People are looking at us. People are pointing at our car." One of my kids notices.

For some unknown reason, I feel embarrassment and the shame for being victimized.

My wife keeps each kid repeating again and again what happened to us to release any trauma, and then we start processing the event together.

The kids are stunned by the fact that these teenagers did what they did, but the proximity in time of the window crashing and Purim make each one of us connect the two making their relevance almost obvious.

"Why did they break our window Mommy?"

"The young people saw Abba in the front seat, and he obviously looks like a religious Jew. They don't like the Jews I suppose," my wife answers.

"So Abba is like Mordechai and these bad people are like Haman," one of our kids simply states.

"Yes. These people are like Haman who wanted to hurt the Jews, nevertheless, Hashem made a miracle for us and nobody was hurt. We just had a personal Purim miracle. Thank you Hashem! The police didn't punish these people, but Hashem will punish them! Or even better, Hashem will make them do Teshuvah!"

The dialogue continues, but the unique comparison between the Purim story and our incident show uncanny parallels. We personalize the story of Purim to this event to our children, and funnily enough, everything fits.

In our Purimesque experience, I was Mordechai, the Jew who Haman hated for not bowing down to him. I rolled down the window asking 'why are doing that,' when they threw the initial little pebble.

The destructive teens were the evil Haman (one person threw the rock, however the rest kept quiet and hid their friend's identity, agreeing with their actions) who threw a rock at our passenger window endangering the lives of our baby and children, G-d forbid.

My wife was Esther. Esther was the heroine whose actions helped save the Jews from Haman's plans and help capture and punish him. My wife's screams finally propelled the cops to chase down and capture the youth. The cops were Achashverush, the authority in the present area.

Just like the attempts of Haman to eradicate Jews was miraculously annulled, so too in our personal Purim story, the potentially threatening rock and shattered glass, miraculously, harmed no one.

৪৩

In the heat of the moment, looking through the shattered window glass, I could see right into the hearts of these teens whose masks gave way in a moment of true baseless hatred.

Right there, in the most unexpected place, SoHo, one of Manhattan's best neighborhoods, under the glitzy billboards and trendy architecture, we were introduced to some of the fruits of this place. Young kids who have been stripped of even basic morality and the ability to distinguish between right from wrong.

I did nothing to provoke them. Even when I rolled down my window, I didn't raise my voice, I didn't get angry.

The girl didn't seem angry either; she just seemed indifferent and cold.

Those kids were dressed in regular American clothes. They weren't religious extremists or part of a hate group as far as I know. They were just ordinary urban New York kids; nevertheless, their evil coldness reeked of Amalek.

The attack was most unexpected and brought to life in a most experiencial manner an old Chasidic lesson:

There is an interesting Purim Halacha that states that if someone reads the Megillah backwards, from the end to the beginning; he hasn't fulfilled his obligation to hear the Megillah on Purim.

The Baal Shem Tov teaches, based on this Halacha, that if someone thinks that the story of the Megillah is a story of some past events that has no relevance or contemporary bearing to one's life now, then he hasn't fulfilled the Mitzvah of 'hearing' the Megilah on Purim.

The shaken, wired and edgy feelings after the attack with its revealed Hashgacha Pratis, Divine Providence, made this Baal Shem Tov teaching reverberate in my mind and made me really see his teaching in the most intimate way. This Purim message just slapped me in the face with a hyper-real state of mind.

Another powerful teaching that jumped into the forefront of my tense mind is from the Arizal based on words from the Megillah itself. On the verse "Hayamim Ha'ele Nizkaim VeNaasim," "these days are commemorated and recreated, (which empower them to) manifest again." Through commemorating and celebrating the holiday by performing its Mitzvos, we actually channel the holy energy inherent in them, drawing them right into our very lives.

The merit of the Mitzvos we performed on Purim surely aided in 'drawing down' our very own miracle of Purim.

However, why did we have to experience this, and not another Jewish family? Why did it happen at all?

A story about Rabbi Aryeh Levin, the Tzadik of Jerusalem, potentially answers this serious inquiry.

Rabbi Levin and his wife were very poor people who did not own many valuable possessions. Their most valuable objects were heirloom china dishes handed down from previous generations.

These dishes were stored on top of a wooden shelf nailed to a wall. One day, the shelf fell to the ground and with it, the precious dishes, which all broke into many pieces.

At the time, Rabbi Levin's wife was at their apartment. She immediately went out looking for her husband to inform him of the news. When she located him, she informed him that a great miracle had happened to them and she had him say Tehilim with her.

Finally, she revealed to him of the great miracle, she told him that there was a terrible decree against their bodies, but instead, Hashem took it out on their dishes!

After it all, my wife and I feel sorry for these kids and see this occurrence as a dirty mark of failure of their educational system and culture. The violent and immoral movies, valueless TV shows, books, toxic music and games that these and countless others ingest daily just desensitize kids and adults alike making the craziest of actions (such as this very one) justifiable. (Other cops we spoke with after the event rationalized it due to these teens being 'bored' or 'unfocused'!)

From somewhere within, I suddenly recall an easy 'remedy' that has been prescribed by the Lubavitcher Rebbe to counteract the G-dless mental space of modern 'culture', the establishment of one minute of prayer in all public schools. One minute to pray to the Creator of the universe, the Maker of all beings would surely reshape the perspective of millions, transforming the world over.

In contrast, the beauty of the Jewish school system's content and the dissemination of the highest values expounded in Torah, make me very proud to be sending my children to these Mentch factories that with Hashem's help, will build people with a compassionate character and a heart of gold.

On the following Monday I filed a police report at the first precinct. They labeled this crime against us as an act of 'reckless endangerment & criminal mischief'. They didn't label this act as a hate crime.

This surprised me, since my daughter did hear the teenager say 'I'm going to smash the Jew's car' just before the attack. Why would they strike our car and not the one in front or behind us? Was it really random? I don't think so.

In addition, by the arrangement of a Crown Heights community activist, I spoke to a community affairs officer who promised to further investigate the incident.

I don't know how proactive they will be and what they will actually do, if anything at all. However, in order for me not to just sit with folded arms and do nothing, I documented the story to share with you.

I infinitely thank you Hashem for saving my family from any harm. I fear to think of other possible outcomes of this affair, Lo Aleino, G-d forbid. May you Hashem continue to protect us.

I wrote this Megillah to publicize the miracle you made for us, our own private Purim miracle during a personal Purim story, within our Purim pogrom. In addition I'd like to thank You for reminding us that even though the Mitzvos of Purim that we performed are behind us, the lesson of Purim is not over yet.

The Purim story will only finish when the coldness of Amalek will be utterly eradicated through each and every one of us, finalized with the imminent arrival of Mashiach in the complete and final redemption, may it manifest this very instant!

ജാ

ONCE

UPON

A

CUSTOMER

hile looking around our Manhattan photo super store, my customer marveled, "I love the human landscape in your store, it's beautiful!"

The flow of people in our retail photo shop, whether a gentle stream or a raging river, is always remarkable. Yet these big numbers are made up of interesting individuals from all around the world. Yes, everybody has a story, and yes, everyone is interesting if you know how to smile and ask the right questions.

I did not know that my job would transport me to China with counter-revolutionary journalists, risking their lives trying to give their people hope; to Antarctica with preservation activists; to exotic locales I have never heard of with in-the-know locals; to ponder the future of education with the president of the New School; to discuss medical research with top specialists; to analyze the human condition with people who survived extreme illness; to talk about art and the photo world with published and award winning photographers.

If you open up just a little, a conversation about a camera product can take you anywhere without the expense or burden of air travel, and even further, inside a stranger's life and heart.

Once, roaming the aisles looking for customers to help, I encountered an elderly lady from Europe. I became her photo gear guide. She wanted a simple pouch for her camera, something unstructured. I showed her a certain neoprene pouch. As she touched it and held it up to her eyes for closer inspection she exclaimed, "It's fantastic!" She wanted me to show her another one, just to compare, which I did. As she saw the other choice she declared with a resonant voice, "No, the other one, the other one is fantastic!"

I show her the color options on my computer screen, she makes her decision, and we wait. The pouch comes; I show her the color to see if she is satisfied - but also to see what word she will use. In her exotic voice laden with emotion she exclaims again, "Yes, it's fantastic!" I couldn't hold myself back from remarking, with a gentle smile on my face, "It's so refreshing to hear somebody use the word fantastic on a $12 pouch, or anything for that matter. Most people just say its ok or it's good, but never have I heard any customer say it's fantastic!"

She smiled, and surprised me with her unexpected answer, which was jeweled with her accent.

"It's how you look at life. If you see life as a gift, you appreciate everything, even a small thing. If not, everything is miserable and gray." Instantly inspired and taken aback, I figured she must be a therapist of some kind, who achieved this appreciation after many years of inner work.

I asked her, "Are you a therapist?"

She replied, "Thank G-d, I'm not; therapists and psychologists just cut people up with analysis, I am an artist! I try to add beauty into this world!"

It was a simple purchase, yet, an inspiring encounter.

Her lens offers a view of the world through which I wish more people could look at their life, exclaiming with appreciation about every little thing, "It's fantastic!"

Another European customer of mine who professionally publishes photography books told me, "I believe a photograph is not finished until it is shared with others, then and only then is it complete."

Likewise, our stories are not complete until shared with others…

ജാൽ

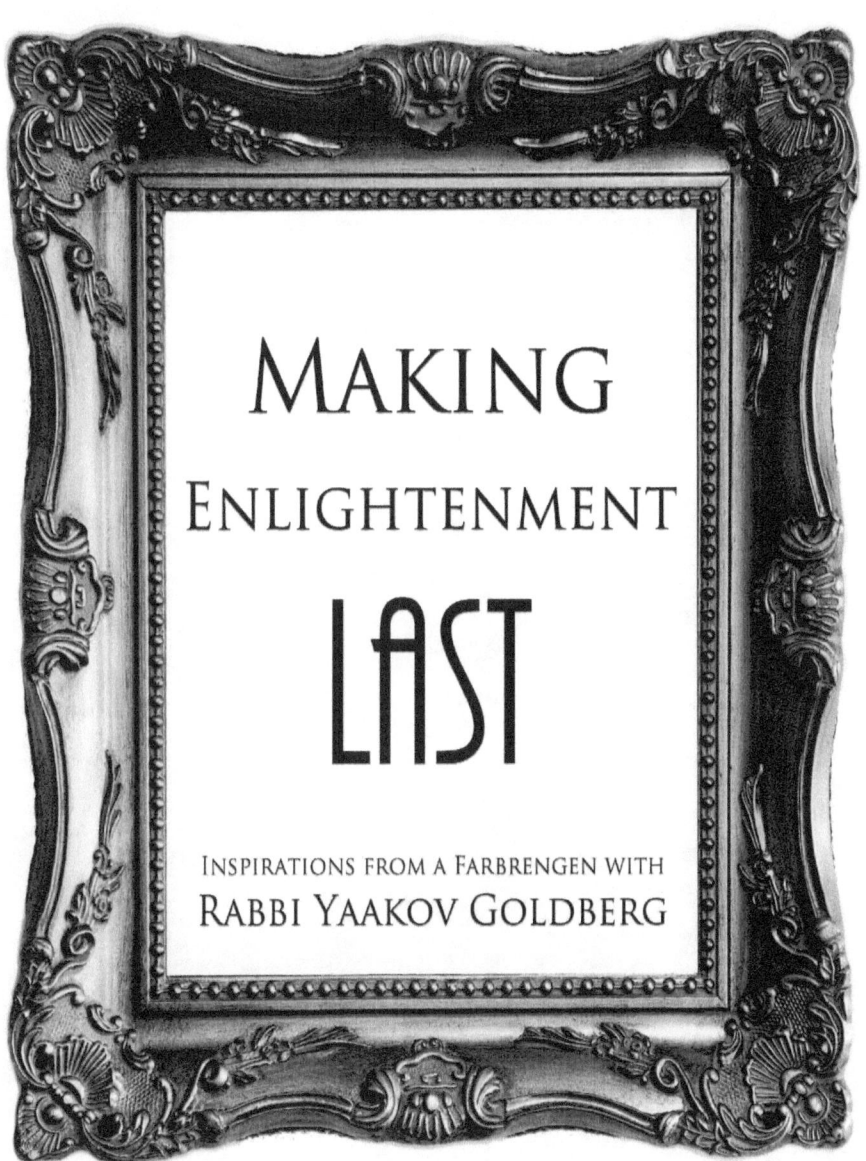

MAKING

ENLIGHTENMENT

LAST

INSPIRATIONS FROM A FARBRENGEN WITH
RABBI YAAKOV GOLDBERG

our zipper is open!" someone once told the Rashag, Rabbi Shmaryahu Gurary (the Rebbe Rayatz's oldest son in law).

"By us Chasidim, everything is open all the time!" The Rashag replied.

I would be more than happy to sit here with my mouth closed; however, the Rebbe said we must speak... Since a Chasidic Farbrengen can accomplish even more than what the Angel Michoel can, therefore we must be completely open and speak. There is much to accomplish.

Even though we hide nothing and have nothing to hide, we can still utilize Remazim, hints, and those who will understand, will understand...

A WARM HOME.
AN ILLUMINATING HOUSE.

A few friends were discussing amongst themselves how to fix some marital problems they were experiencing. They decided to look into the treasure house of Rambam's books for much needed advice.

One individual suggested that the book dealing with Nizikin, Damages, would be the ideal place to look for the appropriate help. His reasoning was that since marriage is combative, fraught with bitter arguments and essentially it's a volatile power struggle in which serious damages resulted, the book of Nizikin would be the right place to find solace for their problems.

A second friend disagreed and suggested that they look in the book of Ahava, Love, since marriage is all about enjoyment and love.

A third fellow suggested that instead of the previously mentioned books, they will find the answer in the book of Nashim, Women, since marriage involves women, an entire book devoted to them should surely dispel any misunderstandings about the other gender's nature.

A fourth guy negated the other three and stated firmly that the answer must be in the book of Kedushah, Sanctification, since marriage requires, and is about, Kedushah, sanctity and holiness.

It goes without saying that the guy who thought marriage is a battle of wills; the fellow who equated marriage to a love affair and also the man that theorized that a good marriage caters to a spouse's human nature were unfortunately unsuccessful in their marriages.

The only one out of this entire bunch whose marriage made it past the challenges was the one who realized that a lasting marriage needs to be a dwelling place of Kedusha, holiness, a subjugation of the self for the benefit of another.

I vividly remember the private audience my wife and I had with the Rebbe on the 19th of Av, 1967. It was just four days after we were engaged on Tu Be'av, the 15th of Av.

In the meeting, the Rebbe blessed us with these words, "Ayir Zalt Oiyfboyen A Varme Uon A Lichtiker Shtub, Uon Mezahl Heren Fon Aiych Besoros Tovos!" "May you build a warm and an illuminating home, and we should hear from you good tidings"

Contemplating these two points I realize that it wasn't only a Bracha, a blessing, but also a directive which contained a formula for a successful marriage.

It isn't enough to have a warm home, a union in which only you are warm and comfortable. The house, the relationship, must be Lichtik, illuminating. A Jewish home should also cast an inspiring aura that affects the outside. Just like the Beis Hamikdash had windows that were 'Shkofim Atomim,' they radiated the light to the outside world, so too with a Jewish house, a personal sanctuary. It should beam outwards with inviting healing rays of light, brightening someone else's experience with a helping hand. This brings about good tidings.

Attaining warmth and light for oneself isn't enough, one must share it with others.

When this condition is met then Kedushah, holiness, dwells there and the couple attains a steadfast, everlasting light.

TODDLERS WITH WHITE BEARDS

"Every Lubavitcher Chasid is 40 years old!" an acquaintance of mine once marveled to me. He was a Mekurav, a congregant friend, of one of the Shluchim, emissaries of the Rebbe.

"What do you mean?" I asked. "There are Chasidim of all age groups...Kids, teenagers, people in their twenties , thirties , fifties , sixties etc."!?"

"What I mean is that every Lubavitcher younger than 40 is as mature as a 40 year old, and that every Lubavitcher older than 40 is as energetic and young as a forty year old!"

In proof of this man's remarkable statement, in Tzeirei Agudas Chabad, the Lubavitch Youth Organization, there are members that are quite elderly, however they are still called 'Tzeirei Chabad', the youth of Chabad.

I've had a white beard for so long I don't even remember what color it was before! Nevertheless, I must say that through the years I happen to have met several Chasidim older than 40, some with white flowing beards, that would be perfectly suited for kindergarten!

Needless to say, just growing older or attaining old age doesn't guarantee acquiring maturity, inspiration or enlightenment...

A FLAME FOR G-D

The Jewish people as a whole are also married; we are married to Hashem.

Our marriage occurred on the mount of Sinai on the historic event of Matan Torah, the giving of the Torah to the Jewish people.

At this most auspicious and significant wedding of all time, Moshe was the Shoshvina DeMalka, the 'best man' representing The King-groom, Hashem. The Shoshvina DeMatronisa, the 'bridesmaid' of the queen, the Jewish people, was Aharon.

The credentials for Moshe might speak for themselves to explain how he merited this prestigious honor; however, a person can wonder and ask: why did Aharon merit such a great honor as being the escort of the Jewish people on this momentous union?

In Likutei Torah (pages 58-60) the Alter Rebbe makes a striking comparison between Avraham Avinu and Aharon that might shed some light on the subject.

Although they both exhibited extraordinary Chesed, kindness, the expression of generosity they displayed varies tremendously.

Avraham as the first Jew spread the consciousness of one G-d versus the prevalent idol-worship in the world at the time. He would make his many guests give thanks to the Creator after partaking meals he served them and compel people to acknowledge the One Supreme Being.

Despite the giving nature of Avraham, if we ask ourselves where are Avraham's students today? Perhaps we can safely say that they are nowhere to be found.

After Avraham died, his students disappeared. He gave and gave and gave some more. He never stopped giving. However, the "Nefashus She'Asu Becharan," the souls Sarah and him have touched and inspired, vanished after the contact with them was severed.

Aharon on the other hand had an entirely different approach.

In the Parsha of Beha'aloscha, it says that Aaron elevated the candles on the menorah when he ignited them with a flame.

The menorah is representative of the Jewish people as a whole, while each one of its seven branches is compared to a certain type of Jew.

The word used to describe this kindling is, Beha'aloscha, which literally means to elevate.

He didn't just light them and leave them, but rather he toiled to elevate them so that they will be a "Shalheves HaOla MeAleha," a flame that burns independently of him.

Aharon exerted effort in bringing out the Jewish people's potential and empowered them through his teachings to be able to keep their inspiration alive by personal inner work on their own.

Interestingly, we are specifically instructed to emulate Aharon.

In Pirkei Avos, the book titled Ethics of our Fathers (1,12), it is stated, "Hevei MeTalmidav Shel Aharon, Ohev

Shalom, VeRodef Shalom, Ohev Es HaBrios, U'Mekarvan LaTorah."

"Be of the disciples of Aharon, loving peace and pursuing peace, loving your fellow creatures, and bringing them close to the Torah."

Unlike Avraham's method, Aharon's path does require of the recipient much effort and toil.

Practically, how does an individual accomplish this? How do we keep the flame for G-d burning?

1. LET THERE BE LIGHT

In the Shul, inside the Shtender, prayer stand, we have stored at least one hundred candles. These candles are real candles, with all the qualities and characteristics of the lit ones used on top of the Shtender by the Davenings, prayers. However, there is one major difference between them, they are missing a flame and therefore they are not illuminating. They need to be sparked and kindled.

People, like candles, need to be kindled, otherwise they will not shine even though the potential is there...

There is a catch though; a prerequisite for this stimulated luminous life experience: an individual has to accept to become lit by an Aharon.

2. HARNESSING DESIRE

The mystic foundational Kabbalah text authored by Rabbi Shimon Bar Yochai, The Zohar, famously states in

Parshas Vayakhel page 110 that the "Moach Shalit Al HaLev," "the mind rules over the heart." However, the heart has some very powerful passions; therefore there is an ongoing struggle between the two as to who will prevail over the other.

There are two possible scenarios that can play out in the duel between the mind and the heart.

In the first scenario the heart leads the mind. A person sees something that jumpstarts the desire of the heart and then the heart introduces the mind to it. This deceptive introduction harbors within it the goal of utilizing the mind, and lures it to find justifications to obey and fulfill the heart's random wanton cravings.

The order of this sequence is Lev - heart, Moach - mind, Kaved - liver. It begins with the heart's wish, and then leads to the mind's justification and excuse, and then the liver's vivifying of the body with blood, signifying action.

The acronym of this spells out Lemech.

Lemech is a character in the Torah who symbolizes the epitome of failure and misfortune having made tragic mistakes that cost a couple of his family members their lives, G-d forbid.

On the other hand, a second scenario is made up of an entirely different order of events. In this second sequence the mind leads the heart. It reasons and decides; concluding with a certain understanding of what is truly good. Then it brings in and involves the heart, harnessing it, to utilize its characteristic trait of desire in order to help fulfill and obey the mind's calculations.

The order of this scenario is Moach - mind, Lev - heart, and Kaved - liver. The mind's conclusions initiate the process; the heart's passion fuels and propels it, and the liver, brings those understandings into action.

The acronym of this sequence spells out Melech, king. By aligning the mind with the Torah, the will of the King, an individual can be triumphant in directing the desire of the heart and one's actions on a G-dly path; such a person is likened to a Melech, a king. This is the meaning of the teaching in Pirkei Avos, the Ethics of Our Fathers, '"Who is a hero? He who rules over his desire…"

The choice between success and failure on our spiritual mission in life is presented to us again and again. It is the choice between losing by following the heart's foolish trappings, being a Lemech, or winning by choosing to align the mind, heart and one's actions with the King's Supernal Will, and thus becoming like a heroic ruler, a Melech, a king.

3. RECHARGING RADIANCE

Last week I got a device called 'cell'. I put it in my pocket and every once in a while it makes a lot of noise and vibrates, insisting I pick it up. I take it in my hand and the screen on it is bright and 'enlightened'. I can so easily reach or be reached now with this phone's instant connection.

A few days after I had this phone I noticed it wasn't making any sounds or vibrating. I took it out of my pocket and noticed its screen wasn't bright and 'enlightened' any more. I told my wife that this new device is probably dead, it isn't producing light anymore. My wife told me that this device has a battery, and that this battery needs to be recharged with a charger.

I opened the box that it came in and found this charging instrument. I plugged this charger to the wall socket before I went to sleep and in the morning I placed the charged battery back in my phone. Amazingly enough, my phone's screen was bright again, emitting light. The next time someone called, it produced its sounds and vibrated excitedly once more.

People are very much like cell phones. When one's battery is charged, when they are 'enlightened', they can be full of radiance emanating vibrations of inspiration to their surrounding environment with one's connection. However, this battery over time does discharge, and when it's drained the person isn't connected anymore, they become dull, quiet and dim. They aren't radiant or enlightened anymore.

How does one regain enlightenment? A person must recharge to reconnect!

How does someone recharge? On special occasions, a person can recharge via participating in a Chasidishe Farbrengen. In addition, on a daily basis, Baalei Batim, married individuals, to maintain their charge and connection, should maintain Kvious Itim LaTorah, set times for learning Torah. Bochurim, students, should keep to their Yeshivah's Sedarim, daily schedule, to keep and increase in radiance.

By utilizing these 'chargers' continuously, an individual's constant connection is certain to last.

A TALE OF TWO KUGELS

A young couple came to a Rov one time, completely upset and emotional, declaring they wanted to divorce. The Rov invited them to sit and tell him all about their marital problems that have led them to this drastic decision. After a little investigating the Rov found the root of the problem.

Apparently the Shabbos Kugel was guilty of coming between these two newlyweds.

In honor of the holy Shabbos, the wife would make a delicious Kugel to fulfill the verse saying, "Me'angeha LeOlam Kavod Inchalo," "those who delight in the Shabbos will inherit eternal glory."

The husband, on the other hand, was meticulous about the Halacha, law, in the Shulchan Aruch which states that a person should taste from the foods of Shabbos on Erev Shabbos, the Friday afternoon before. He was especially enthusiastic about it since he wanted to fulfill, "To'ameha Chaim Zacho," "those who taste from these (Shabbos foods on Erev Shabbos) will merit eternal life."

He was quite adamant about beautifying this Mitzvah inspired by the verse "Vegam Ha'Ohavim D'Vareha Gedula Bacharu," "even those who love its precepts have chosen a great portion."

It wasn't enough for him to have just a little piece... A great big portion or even two or three big pieces weren't enough either... He ate the whole Kugel!

The woman was upset since she had no Kugel to serve on Shabbos. The husband was upset because he wanted to eat the entire Kugel Erev Shabbos.

The Rov thought about this major dilemma and then advised the couple:

"The solution for this is a simple one. Why don't you cook two Kugels?! One will be for Erev Shabbos and one will be for Shabbos. This way both of you will be happy!"

This year is 5773 years since creation; we are undeniably living in an era that is deemed Erev Shabbos, the afternoon before the Shabbos of creation, the Messianic Era.

This ultimate Shabbos is coming very soon and gets closer and closer; however we are still holding in the time of Erev Shabbos.

During the Messianic Era there will be an abundant amount of delicacies served. These delicacies are the revelations of the inner aspects of Torah, its inner dimension, an amazing revelation of G-dliness. It's a Mitzvah to eat the delicacies of Shabbos before Shabbos. These delicacies, these revelations, are served in Chasidic teachings.

Hashem has generously 'cooked' and created two 'Kugels'; one for Shabbos and one for Erev Shabbos. There is no doubt that the 'Kugel' for Shabbos is phenomenal; however a similar 'Kugel' is being served now on the platter of Chasidus.

We don't have to fear of eating the entire 'Kugel'. Hashem has made another one for Shabbos. Each one of us is invited to eat the 'Kugel' prepared especially for Erev Shabbos, pure revelations of G-dliness, now.

We are given the delicacy of Chasidus for us to consume completely!

AN ESSENTIAL REVELATION !

The Talmud (Shabbos, 95, a) demystifies the word 'Anochi' which appears in the very first of the Aseres HaDibros, the ten commandments: "Anochi Hashem Elukecha," "I am the Lord, your G-d." It reveals the acronym that these letters stand for, "Anochi Nafshi Kasavis Yahavis," "I placed myself in these writings."

Hashem declares that he puts his very 'self' into the Torah! If we take a moment to reflect and internalize what that actually means... By learning Torah we are dealing with the Creator Himself intimately 'face to face'!

When we learn Torah we are connecting and uniting with Hashem's Ratzon HaElyon, Supernal Will. When we learn Chasidus, the inner aspect of Torah, we are grappling with the inner aspects, the essence of Hashem!

Isn't this just astounding?! Isn't this awe inspiring?!

Some people emphasize that the reward for Torah and Mitzvos will be "LeAsid Lavo," "in the future to come," by the complete redemption, or in "Gan Eden."

Practically, that means that their learning of the Torah and the performance of the Mitzvos are like an unwanted burden which the individual will perform just because of the reward he will get later. A practical example of this could be an uninspired worker who is stuck in a job he doesn't like yet holds onto it only for the paycheck.

Chasidus revealed a completely different perspective in which the emphasis is that the reward is now!

"Schar Mitzvah Mitzvah," "the reward of a Mitzvah is the fulfilling of the Mitzvah itself." When we learn Torah the 'Anochi' dwells within us and is like consumed bread which becomes one with our flesh; this is an amazing union with the Almighty.

Even though nowadays we don't sense it, the learning of Torah equals and elicits a revelation of Hashem.

We are 'paid' now; the 'payment' being the amazing privilege to actually fulfill the Master of The Universe's Supernal Will. What an incredible fact!

When a person is learning Torah that is a great accomplishment! When an individual learns, he transforms a mere day into a successful one.

What greater accomplishment and success in a person's day is there if not for involving oneselves with Hashem personally?

You don't have to wait for a fuller grasp in some future time; you can start to taste the labor of your fruits today, when you learn Torah, right this very moment!

In light of the Chasidic teachings on the subject, the question a person should ask themselves is not, "did I learn Torah today or not?" The question should be, "how many times did I learn Torah today?"

BEYOND DOUBT OR REASON

A certain store in Manhattan occupied an entire block and rose up several stories high. One time its director met up with another director of a similar megastore in the former USSR. As these two started talking, their curiosities about each other's businesses naturally led to comparisons.

"How many employees do you have?" asked the Russian director.

"Well, let's see. The store has ten floors and each floor has around one hundred employees. So in total we have approximately one thousand employees." The American director answered.

"What do you mean by one thousand employees? What do you need so many workers for? In Russia we also have a gigantic store just as big as yours in America; however, we manage with only ten workers, one for every floor." The Russian director stated.

"How can you manage with only one employee on every floor?" The American director wondered.

"Well, the way it works is that the customer comes in and goes to the appropriate floor depending on what he wants. As an example, a customer asks the salesperson 'Do you have a chair?' and the salesperson says 'Niet!' No! Another customer goes to another floor for pants and asks if they sell pants and the answer is a firm 'Niet! No! We don't have it!' In your American store it's different. A customer comes in, and let's says they want a suit, they are directed to the right area. There a salesperson asks what kind of suit, what material and what color. Then they will show the customer several options...For such an operation you definitely need so much staff on hand. But with us, we just nip it in the bud. We say we don't have it and that is it! The conversation is finished..."

The second chapter of Pirkei Avos starts off with the words "Rebbe Omer," "the Rebbe says." After that it continues with many golden teachings, but the very first words are "the Rebbe says."

This detail directly applies to our approach to the Rebbe, his teachings, directives and campaigns. The reason of our adherence should simply be because "The Rebbe says!" Similar to the blunt Russian salesperson's response.

We shouldn't depend on our limited and biased understanding, picking and choosing what seems good to us. Unlike the American store, there is no need to extend great customer service to doubts, delving into elaborate debates and explanations searching if a teaching or Hora'a, directive, is perfectly tailored to our personal comfort zones or proclivities. We should shed our personal agendas.

It's in our very best interest to subdue ourselves under the authority of the Rebbe. When we nullify ourselves to the Rebbe, it helps us to be nullified to what the Rebbe is nullified to... When we bond ourselves with the Rebbe, this enables us to be bonded with what the Rebbe is bonded with.

We must realize the Rebbe's parental far reaching vision truly encompasses 'the big picture' beyond that which we can fathom. We can compare this to a child who must trust that the parent knows best even though he might not fully understand the reason. If a child questions the parents on every little thing, as is so common here in America, it could be quite disastrous.

The Rebbe is our father and he is our mother! We are given the merit to choose to be a smart child and trust the Rebbe's words without question. We can be assured that his lead is for the ultimate best in general, and also in particular, for us on a personal level.

Any contrary claim, doubt or hesitation should be quickly stumped with the firm answer "because the Rebbe says so!" Likewise, as we follow the Rebbe's path, we shouldn't do so because of our grasp or comprehension in whatever matter, but solely because "the Rebbe says so!"

TORAH VISION

A Chasid from the crowd randomly asks, "Rabbi Goldberg do you have a television in your house?"

I do not have a television in my home. The reason behind this is because the television is not MY vision.

If it exclusively portrayed the Torah view, Chasidic topics and perspectives or the Rebbe's vision, then I would have one.

But since the television broadcasts viewpoints that are foreign to and altogether contrary to what I believe, I do not have one in my house!

A PERMISSIBLE DESECRATION

It is written that "Shina BeShabbos Ta'anug," "sleeping on Shabbos is a pleasure." Many people enjoy observing this special 'Mitzvah' and sleep during the Shabbos afternoon. When an occasional Farbrengen happens along on a Shabbos, a person could be tempted to forgo the Farbrengen altogether, since the Mitzvah of sleeping on Shabbos is so great and the Farbrengen would become a clear obstacle to its fulfillment.

Another Shabbos Halacha, law, states that you may violate the Shabbos to save a life. The reasoning behind this is that you are violating one Shabbos in order to enable the individual to observe many Shabbosos in the future.

We can apply this Halacha to those cajoled by this sleep reason who either leave a Farbrengen early or simply didn't show up because of it. To them we can say, "Violate your Shabbos, your special Mitzvah of sleeping, so you can enable having many more inspired Shabbosos!"

In addition to their great adherence to this Mitzvah of sleeping, other 'holy' excuses can come up backed up with substantial legitimate claims such as "it is very important to spend time with one's wife and kids" or "my wife will miss me" etc.

To calm these kinds of claims, I can assure you that by participating in a Chasidishe Farbrengen or a Shiur, a Torah class, not only will your family survive and not think less of you for being absent, on the contrary. Since you will be enlivened and awakened by it, your wife and children will admire you!

A LASTING RESOLUTION

A certain Rov's wife liked listening in on her husband's various Dinei Torah, case judgments. Just as she listened in on many previous cases, she was eavesdropping attentively to a particular case to her great bewilderment.

Two men came into the Rov's office to resolve their business altercation.

Levi started, detailing his side of the story at length. After Levi finished his account the Rov thought about what he had said and then presented them his judgment.

"Levi after thinking about what you told me I've come to the conclusion that you are right!" The Rov concluded.

"Wait. How could you judge in Levi's favor before listening to my side of the story?" Shimon asked.

"Don't worry. We are not finished yet... Let's hear your side of the story Shimon." The Rov asked.

Shimon proceeded to explain the matter as he experienced it after which the Rov pondered and clearly was digesting the information.

"Shimon, I was thinking about what you said and I believe that you are right too." The Rov settled.

After both businessmen left the Rov's office, his wife who was listening the whole while, entered it.

"I heard the entire case and I must say I'm puzzled. I don't understand. How could both Shimon and Levi be right at the same time?" she asked curiously.

The Rov gazed out of the office window and thought for a little while before answering his wife, "you are also right!"

At a conclusion of a Farbrengen we must attempt to pinpoint something to hold onto and take away from it to implement it into our lives 'LeMa'aseh BePoal,' into the realm of action.

One person can take this, a second person can take that, while a third can take another, yet, they are all right.

Regardless what you choose to take with you, I'd like to especially highlight the importance of learning Chasidus! Besides being literally a Giloy Elokos, a revelation of G-dliness, it personally solidifies and internalizes the consciousness of "Ani Hashem Elokechem: Emes," "I am the Lord your G-d: the truth." When a person learns Chasidus, then that day is truly a complete day of special achievement.

It is vital to learn Chabad Chasidus every single day!

৪৩৫৫

GLOSSARY

Amidah Prayer – (Lit. the standing prayer) the centerpiece of the three daily prayers (wherein we beseech G-d for all our personal and communal needs, the weekday Amidah); Also known as Shmoneh Esre, or Eighteen, based on the original number of prayers it included. Now there are nineteen. Also known as the Tefilah, or the prayer.

Baal Teshuvah - (lit. "Master of return") A person who 'returns' to G d in repentance, after transgressing the Torah's commandments either willful or unknowingly; a Jew of 'secular' or not fully observant background, who has decided to undertake full Torah observance.

Bima(h) – the podium on which the Torah is read in the synagogue, usually situated at its center. It is representative of the altar that was in the Holy Temple in Jerusalem.

Chabad - is an acronym for Chochmah, intellect (which refers to conception of an idea), Bina, understanding (which refers to integrating and developing the idea) and Daas, knowledge (which refers to actualizing the idea). This acronym is also the name of the Chasidic branch started by the Alter Rebbe, Rabbi Shneur Zalman of Liadi, which delves into the cognitive and intellectual depths of the inner and mystical aspects of Torah, emphasizing the service of Hashem through deep intimate knowledge.

Chasidut/Chasidus – A Jewish movement started by the Baal Shem Tov which revolutionized the Jewish landscape by emphasizing devotion to Hashem by the learning of the esoteric aspects of Torah. The goal in revealing the secrets of Torah to all Jews, not just the scholars, is directly connected with the rectification of the world, and as a preparation for the coming of Mashiach. The teachings brought forth by the Chasidic Rebbes are also called Chasidut/Chasidus.

Chasidim/ Chasid – A follower and student of a Chasidic Rebbe.

Daf – An entire page of the Talmud (Gemara) that comprises of both front and back sides of the page.

Dvar Torah – An insight or inspirational thought expressing an aspect from the Torah.

Fast of Gedalyah - fast on the third of Tishrei, commemorating the assassination of Gedaliah ben Achikam, governor of the First Jewish Commonwealth in the Holy Land after the destruction of the first holy Temple in Jerusalem; after this assassination, Jewish autonomy tragically came to an end. This fast was established soon after the fast for the destruction of the holy Temple on the ninth of Av, Tisha Be'av, was established with an inner message that the death of the righteous is likened to the destruction of the holy Temple.

Farbrengen – a Chasidic gathering permeated with exchanges of Torah thoughts, singing and Chasidic stories.

Gemara – a common "nickname" for the Talmud (the central Jewish thought compilation texts; for more see Talmud). More specifically the term Gemara (literally to learn, or learning) is the discussions which elucidate the germinal statements of law (Mishnayot) collectively known as the Mishnah.

Geula Hashlema - the complete redemption

Hafatza – Jewish in-reach (and outreach) to other Jews with the set goal to empower and inspire greater Jewish awareness and observance.

Halacha (Plural: **Halachos**) – Literally "the pathway," is the name for either the body of Jewish law or of a single law.

Kavanah – The intention or concentration of the mind on the Mitzvah or prayer.

Koshea – A complex Halachic question.

Kabalas Ole – The acceptance of the yoke of heaven.

Krias Shema – Literally the Recitation of the Shema (to hear); the daily declaration of faith, recited in the morning and evening prayers and before retiring for the night

Kvius (Kvius Itim) – The establishment of regular set times to learn Torah, daily and weekly.

Illuy - Torah prodigy

Parsha/h – The weekly Torah portion.

Pe'ah – A tractate of the Mishnayos that deal with the gifts due to the poor when fields, vineyards or trees are harvested, and the laws of giving charity in general. It is the second tractate of the Seder Zeraim, "Order of Seeds."

L'Chaim – Literally "to life" is a common way to begin a toast to one another.

Matan Torah - The historic event of giving of the Torah to the Jewish people by the Creator, at Har Sinai, Mount Sinai.

Melamed - A teacher of Jewish studies

Mesiras Nefesh – An act of self-sacrifice.

Meshuganes - Crazy people!

Mishnah - The first compilation of the oral law, authored by Rabbi Yehudah HaNasi (approx. 200 C.E.); the germinal statements of law elucidated by the Gemara, together with which they constitute the Talmud; also, a single statement of law from this work.

Ma'amer - a Chasidic discourse delving into the esoteric and mystical depths of the Torah.

Masmidim – Diligent scholars or students.

Mosad – An institution.

Mishcan - The Tabernacle.

Neila – Literally 'The closing" (of the gates of Heaven) is the last of five prayers of the day of Yom Kippur

Neshamah – The soul.

Poretz - A land baron.

Rambam (Maimonides) - Acronym for Rabbi Moshe ben Maimon, one of the most important figures in the history of Torah scholarship. On his gravestone this saying is inscribed: "From Moses to Moses, none arose like Moses." To this day, students pore over his scholarly works.

Rebbe – As expounded upon by the Rebbe himself regarding his Rebbe (Rabbi Yosef Yitzchok, the 6th Lubavitcher Rebbe) a Rebbe (Chabad Rebbe) is more than just a man of self-sacrifice, Torah genius, lofty character, prophetic ability, miracle worker, etc. The primary aspect of a Rebbe is that he is a "Nassi," which is broadly defined as, "A head of the multitude of Israel." He is their "head" and their "mind," their source and channel of vitality. Through attachment to him, they are bound and united with their source, and the source of their source, up to their ultimate source on high. (See more at Igros Kodesh, Volume 3; page 331-2)

Rosh Hashanah – Literally "the head of the year." It is a solemn New Year holiday which falls on the first two days of the Hebrew month of Tishrei. (This is also the beginning of the Ten Days of Repentance climaxing at the 10th of the month in Yom Kipur.)

Seder - The day's schedule or ordered routine

Sefer – A book of Torah content, therefore considered to be holy.

Shaloch Manos – (Mishloach Manos) literally, "sent foods." This is one of the main Mitzvos of Purim which comprises of sending gifts of food specifically during Purim day, at least 2 ready to eat items to at least one friend.

Shidduch – The name for a marriage arrangement.

Shlichus – The mission to reach and inspire every Jew on the globe to ascend in Jewish knowledge and observance. This can also mean one's life mission in the world, that of learning Torah and performing Mitzvos

Shulchan Aruch – Literally, "a set table". This is the standard code of Jewish law compiled by Rabbi Yosef Karo. Together with its many commentaries, it is the most authoritative and widely accepted compilation of Jewish law ever written.

Shushan Purim – In certain walled cities, like Jerusalem, Purim is observed on the 15th of Adar instead of the 14th of Adar the date of observance everywhere else. This is to commemorate that in the walled town of Shushan, where the battles between the Jews and their enemies lasted one more day, the original Purim celebration was held on the 15th of Adar, not the 14th.

Therefore the 15th of the month is called "Shushan Purim" and it's a day of great joy and celebration, also in those places where the 15th isn't observed as the actual Purim.

Shas – "Shisha Sedarim," the six orders. The Shas is a traditional nickname for the Talmud which is sectioned to six general subjects. *See Talmud…*

Talmud – (Lit. to study or learning) the fundamentally central text compendium of Jewish law and thought; its' tractates mainly comprise the discussions collectively known as the Gemara, which elucidate the germinal statements of law (Mishnayot) collectively known as the Mishnah; when unspecified, it's referred to as the Talmud Bavli, the edition developed in Babylonia, and edited at the end of the fifth century C.E.; the Talmud Yerushalmi is the edition compiled in the Land of Israel at the end of the fourth century C.E.

Tkias – The name for the blows (sounds) of the Shofar .

Yidden – The Yiddish name for the Jewish people.

Yomim Tovim – Literally "Good Days," the name for Jewish holidays.

Yom Kippur – The holiest day of the Jewish year, the Day of Atonement, which occurs on the 10th day of the month of Tishei.

Yetzer Hara – Literally: the evil inclination.

Zion /Tzion – Is a name for Jerusalem, the land of Israel and the Jewish people. Additional meanings are: a sign showing the way and the innermost aspect of the soul.

ಬಂ

A PARTIAL PUBLICATION HISTORY

Jump into the Fire
1) ChabadInfo.Com, Tammuz 5771, July 2011.
Titled: *'What's the Sacrifice for Jewish Education?'*
2) Beis Moshiach, 6 Tammuz 5771, July 8 2011

A Child, On the Street, In the Night
1) Collive.Com, Nov 26, 2011
2) CrownHeights.Info, Nov 27, 2011

Cleaning Lady Alert!
1) Collive.Com, March 7th, 2010, titled: *'Our Cleaning Lady Stole'*.
2) Shmais, March 8, 2010, titled: *'If you have a cleaning lady working in your home read this!'*
3) CrownHeights.Info, March 9th, 2010. Titled: 'Our Cleaning Lady Who Stole From Us'
4) TheYeshivahWorld.Com, March15th, 2010.
5) Hamodia, Weekend edition
6) TheLakewoodView.com, Nov 29th, 2010, Titled: *'Our Cleaning Lady Stole- One Family's Experience'*

Gold and Silver
Originally published on the Judaism website, Chabad.Org

PhotoSynthesis
B&H Snapshot, May 2010, titled: 'Photosynthesis: Living the B&H Way.'

The Answer for Everything
1) Chabad.Info, 11 Shvat 5773, January 22, 2013,
titled: *'Being "Chassidish" Is Not Enough'*.
2) Beis Moshiach, 20th of Tammuz, 5773, June 28
2013

Bloody Winter
CrownHeights.Info, January 11, 2012

The Human Camera
B&H Snapshot:
1) January 2011, Part 1 titled 'The Human Camera'.
2) February 2011, Part 2 titled 'Changes Come from
Within'.

Seeing G-dliness
1) CrownHeights.Info, June10th 2012, titled: *'Seeing
G-dliness: A Collection Of Chasidic Tales.'*
2) Chabad.Info, 20 Sivan 5772, June 10th 2012,
Titled: *'Seeing G-dliness, And Other Stories'*
3) Beis Moshiach, July 4th, 2012
4) Collive.Com, June 10th, 2012, Titled: *'Tales from a
Farbrengen'*.

The King's Friend
1) Originally published on the Judaism website,
Chabad.Org
2) The Scroll, The Chabad.Org Weekly Reader
publication, June 14, 2013

The Art of Hugging a Tree
CrownHeights.Info, July 5 2011, titled: *'The Art of Hugging A Tree- A Gimmel Tammuz Diary'*

What Is A Farbrengen?
1) Collive.Com, Nov 26, 2010, Title: *'A Farbrengen Is Not A Speech'*
2) Beis Moshiach, 26 Kislev 5771, Dec 3 2010

Our Purim Pogrom
1) CrownHeights.Info, March 15th, 2012
2) ColLive.Com, March 15th 2012, titled: *'Our Family's Purim Pogrom'*
3) Chabad.Info, 22 Adar 5772, March 16, 2012, titled *'Pogrom in Manhattan and Useless NYPD Cops'*

Once Upon A Customer
1) B&H Snapshot, September, 2009
2) Chabad.Org

Making 'Enlightenment' Last
Beis Moshiach, 13 Tammuz, 5773, June 21 2013, titled *'Recharge Yourself'*.

ৰক্ষ

FARBRENGEN DATES

The Answer For Everything
A collage of inspirations from several Farbrengens &
Hitdabruyot circa 5764/5 (2004/5)

The Wealthy Family
Yud Tes Kislev Farbrengen, 5766 (2006)

What is a Farbrengen?
From the Hadar Hatorah Alumni Melave Malka
19th Kislev Farbrengen 5770 (2010)

Jump Into The Fire
From a Farbrengen celebration of Hadar Hatorah
Yeshivah's 49th anniversary, Shabbos Shlach, 5771 (2011)

Seeing G-dliness
From a Farbrengen celebration of Hadar Hatorah
Yeshivah's 50th Anniversary, Shabbos Naso, 5772 (2012)

Making Enlightenment Last
From a Farbrengen celebration of Hadar Hatorah
Yeshivah's 51st Anniversary, Shabbos Baha'aloscha, 5773 (2013)

ෂෟඋ

NOTEWORTHY CREDITS

Rabbi Yaakov Goldberg is an admired and beloved educator who merited to be called a Lamdan, a diligent scholar, by the Lubavitcher Rebbe. He is the Rosh Yeshivah of Hadar Hatorah and a Meshiv in Tomchei Tmimim Yeshivah in 770 where he answers questions on all Shas and Halacha.

Hadar Hatorah (also known as Yeshivas Kol Yaakov Yehudah Hadar Hatorah Rabbinical Seminary) is the world's first Ba'al Teshuvah Yeshivah (an authentic Jewish learning center designed and dedicated for the enrichment of Jewish men with little or no formal background in Jewish education or observance), literally transforming thousands of lives since its founding in 1962.

Hadar Hatorah offers fulltime and part time curriculums as well as shorter inspiring educational retreats such as Yeshivah Shabbos and the ten day Yeshivahcation, both in Brooklyn during the winter and in their breathtaking Catskill Mountain campgrounds during the summer.

Telephone: **718 735 0250**
Website: **HadarHatorah.Org**

Rabbi Yosef Avraham HaLevy Heller assumed the role as member of the rabbinical court in a community election, following the death of Rabbi Zalman Shimon Dvorkin, the community's first chief rabbi close to three decades ago. The same election appointed Rabbis Yehuda Kalmen and Avraham Osdoba, establishing the Crown Heights Beth Din, rabbinical court.

In addition, He holds the position of the Rosh Kollel, head of Kollel Menachem, the central Chabad Lubavitch Kollel, Yeshivah for married men. (It is customary in Chabad circles for men to study in Kollel for at least one year after getting married.)

Kollel Menachem – the central Chabad Lubavitch Kollel, located in Crown Heights, was established by the Rebbe in 1962, under the aegis of Machne Israel and the Mazkirus.

It has since become a renowned institution of advanced Torah study serving young students from around the world. Kollel Fellows have assumed prominent Rabbinic positions on Shlichus, in the Rabbinate or lay leadership in Jewish communities around the globe.

Rabbi Chaim Shalom Deitch is the Rosh Kollel of the Tzemach Tzedek Kollel in the old city of Jerusalem. Since his youth, he was considered a Torah Illui, genius prodigy, and is considered to be one of the world's foremost authorities on the Alter Rebbe's Shulchan Aruch. He is also a charismatic teacher of Chasidus whose Farbrengens are truly in a class of their own and are a big draw for many.

Tzemach Tzedek Kollel is a landmark in the old city of Jerusalem. In 1856 it was erected by Lubavitch Chasidim who migrated to Jerusalem from Chevron, where they were persecuted by their Arab neighbors. The building of the Kollel was strongly encouraged by the third Lubavitcher Rebbe, Rabbi Menachem Mendel of Lubavitch, after whom it is named.

It currently hosts a vibrant Kollel with students from the world over, a synagogue for Shabbos and holidays and various outreach programs through its Chabad house.

Address: **31 Chabad Street, Old City of Jerusalem**

୫୦ଔ

- *To help support* **Hadar Hatorah Yeshivah** *with a donation please contact:* **HadarHatorah.Org.**

- *To help support* **Kollel Menachem** *or the* **Tzemach Tzedek Kollel** *with a contribution please contact:* **Lubavitch.Com.**

୫୦ଔ

ABOUT THE AUTHOR

Rabbi Bentzion Elisha received his Smicha, Rabbinical ordination, from the Central Lubavitch Yeshivah of Tomchei Tmimim (770) in Crown Heights, Brooklyn, New York.

His writings are bold and innovative contributions to the world of authentic Jewish literature and culture. Rabbi Elisha is a prolific producer of original thought provoking articles and riveting stories, eye opening transformational Torah adaptations and soul stirring songwriting. The author's unique perspective, and distinct expressive style, has been showcased and widely published in various leading publications and websites.

In addition, he is an acclaimed artist who has won several awards for his creative photography by famed imaging giants which include: Canon USA Inc. and Sigma Corporation of America.

He resides in Brooklyn, NY, with his family.

80QR

*In prayer for the immediate
healing and a healthy long life of*

Mazal bas Tamar

Menachem Mendel HaKohen ben Devorah Shifra

৪০০৪

In the merit of

Tamar bas Mashiach Z"L
Simon ben Yedidyah Z"L
Bentzion ben Yitzchak Z"L
Leah bas Moshe Z"L

Chaya bas Shlomo Z"L
Dovid ben Israel Z"L
Avraham ben Yosef Z"L
Bat Sheva bas Boruch Z"L

Devorah bas Simon Z"L
Moshe ben Bentzion Z"L
Rivkah bas Shalom Z"L

Menashe Dov Yaakov ben Moshe Z"L
Binyamin Eliezer ben Dovid Z"L
Paz Feivel ben Dovid Z"L

৪০০৪